VINH LONG

VINH LONG

Harvey Meyerson

WITH AN INTRODUCTION BY
CONGRESSMAN JOHN V. TUNNEY

*Illustrated with maps
by Adam Nakamura*

HOUGHTON MIFFLIN COMPANY BOSTON

1970

*This book is dedicated to the memory
of my father, Dr. Sol Meyerson,
with love and reverence*

It is also dedicated to all those
who lack grace under pressure, but who
stick it out just the same

Modern man can know himself only insofar as he can become conscious of himself.

CARL GUSTAV JUNG

Acknowledgments

THE YOUNG American lieutenants and captains in Vinh Long were as fine a group as I have met. To them a special word of thanks, as well as to those American civilians who shared their thoughts with me.

Ray Coffey's hospitality during stops in Saigon and the encouragement of Dorothy de Santillana and David Halberstam over a lonely two and a half years helped make it all much easier.

Tom Buchanan's sensitive editorial criticism was invaluable.

To the members of the History of American Civilization Department at Brandeis University I owe a debt of gratitude for their kind forbearance during the final writing stages.

As for my mother, Ida, and my sister and brother-in-law, Linda and René Tillich, words won't do.

Preface

THE IDEA FOR THIS BOOK came from George Orwell's "Homage to Catalonia." When Orwell covered the Spanish Civil War, he concentrated on the province of Catalonia, serving with a Republican unit in the field there and observing the turmoil in Barcelona. Without financial backing, without credentials, without access to men of influence, without a Big Picture perspective, Orwell still managed in a few months to arrive at an understanding of what was happening in Spain that went beyond the most "informed" reporting on the war.

It struck me that virtually no one who reported on the war in Vietnam had stood still for any length of time, like Orwell. Everyone seemed to be moving — from this battlefield to that pacification project, round and round. Maybe something could be learned from picking a spot, then standing still for a while.

In January 1967, I gave up a post as a foreign correspondent for the *Chicago Daily News* and moved from Paris to Vinh Long, a province in the Mekong Delta in South Vietnam. I remained in Vinh Long through the summer, then went to Honolulu to write, then back to Vinh Long for February and March of 1968, then to Honolulu, to Cambridge, Massachusetts, writing, and, finally, once more to Vinh Long in December 1968.

It did not take long for me to become convinced that by concentrating on a single province I had succeeded in avoiding a dangerous snare. So much is happening in Vietnam, simultaneously, at so many different places, on so many different levels, that the panoramic approach — dominant in the literature on Vietnam — has the effect of harnessing the observer's senses to a powerful centrifugal pull that sends impressions and conclusions spinning outward. The panoramic observer is writing from no context capable of holding a piece of information, fixing it under a light, then moving in more information, comparing, accepting, rejecting, until a measure of understanding can be breathed into his work. The result is that insights quickly become diffused, like bursts in a psychedelic light show.

A single province provides the missing context. Insights that in the Big Picture environment explode outward now become susceptible to containment, and even dissection. Statistical measurements can be examined critically at the source. The events of yesterday, last week, last month, can be correlated directly with the events of today, tomorrow, next month. The observer who concentrates on one province develops a mastery of his material not possible on the scale of the Big Picture. In effect, he exchanges independence of movement for independence of mind.

The province observer must watch himself, however. American workers on the scene tend to regard their province as a world unto itself. For the resident observer it is not that but, again, a _context_. He must move out of the province from time to time and examine it from a distance — at 9th ARVN Division headquarters, Vinh Long is one province in a "world" of six provinces; at IV Corps headquarters, it is one province in sixteen; at the United States Mission in

Saigon, it is one province in forty-five. Each view offers new perspective and new understanding.

So, too, does the view from America. Just living in Vietnam works on an observer's senses. The bizarre environment — languid, violent, foreign, at times surreal — conditions his responses. He may be influenced in his own judgment by the hopes or, in some cases, the cynicisms of Americans around him. It becomes important to get away entirely, then to return, as if one is studying a way of life that cannot be understood before it has been experienced, yet cannot be wholly understood while it is being experienced.

It came to me as something of a surprise to learn that even the bureaucratic institutions in Vietnam — the sources of "hard" statistical information — militate against understanding. One could ask the same statistical question of five different persons at five different echelons and get five different sets of "authoritative" statistics.[1] Obtaining a true picture was like working out a two-step jigsaw puzzle. The first step was to find the pieces. In this respect, the province base proved especially useful. It served as a repository for all the seemingly unrelated and sometimes contradictory bits and pieces. Here they could be checked one against the other. As time passed, the reliable information pyramided and the picture grew clearer.

At first, the book was structured as a narrative, with one chapter flowing into the next. This technique was abandoned after I felt myself falling into another snare which can develop when, in attempting to give living expression to certain forces, the writer allows his narrative to develop a

---

[1] I had thought the wartime climate of secrecy would present the greatest technical obstacle to my work. Though secrecy prevailed (it took verbal requests to twelve different persons plus four written requests over a six-month period to obtain declassification of a single document), the main problem, it turned out, was finding a way through that bureaucratic maze.

life of its own; now a set of *literary* requirements begin to exert a subtle and in some ways corrupting influence. To avoid the literary snare the book was blocked out into five unconnected narrative parts. Then, for one of the five (Part One), the narrative was abandoned altogether. I mention all this in order to emphasize that whenever the choice was between narrative flow or choppy clarity and coherence, the latter won out, deliberately.

The first part is the story of a pacification project. It shows how Americans were unable to see what was happening around them: they had made themselves dependent on an illusion that demanded constant reinforcement. Part Two tells of a battle. The purpose is to give the reader a feeling for Delta warfare at its most intense, explain the Viet Cong system of organization and attack, and offer some indication of the truly extraordinary interweaving of U.S.-ARVN[2] responsibilities; as the reader will see, ARVN in Vinh Long has been made *organically dependent* on American support. Building on this foundation, the third part, an account of the 1967–68 "Tet Offensive," moves in for a closer examination of U.S.-ARVN and the Viet Cong. Part Four views the impact of the war on one American and, indirectly, on his Vietnamese associates. Those who argue that the Vietnam war is the same as the Korean War or World War II, except that Vietnam is getting more living color coverage, are asked to pay particular attention to this chapter and to try to imagine a parallel experience emerging out of World War II or Korea. Part Five reports on my final visit to Vinh Long.

Buttressing the text, like the proverbial base of the iceberg, is a great deal of omitted material. To anyone with a sense of irony, Vietnam offers an anecdotal gold mine. He who taps this treasure too frequently usually ends up with a collection

2 ARVN: Army of Vietnam. GVN: Government of Vietnam.

of titillating yet redundant sketches. Dozens of such anec-
dotes were stricken out. The criterion for selection was not
how amusing or absurd the anecdote but how much it contributed to understanding. The same goes for statistical information. The chapter on the Tet Offensive was written
after more than a thousand Viet Cong incidents were cata-
loged, graphed, charted, and plotted on a map. Yet the
reader gets no graphs or tables because, at least in the case
of Vietnam, they do not illuminate — they hypnotize; they
take on an independent existence, drawing the reader into
a mathematical dream world where figures come to exist more
and more in relation to each other and less and less in relation to their living origins. In short, every effort has been
made to burn out the sometimes hypnotic irrelevancies and
assign some coherence to the remaining essentials.

The selection of a province in the Delta was deliberate.
Only the Delta has been spared from a U.S.-North Vietnamese confrontation. During the period of this study, no
North Vietnamese ground units were operating south of the
Mekong River, according to United States Army intelligence.
Nor were there any United States divisions chewing up the
countryside.[3] What exists is an indigenous Viet Cong supplied primarily from the outside, just like its ARVN oppo-
nents.[4] This measure of consistency is important because
my objective is not so much to gauge who is winning or losing
as it is to understand the *nature* of American involvement.
Not: Will Khe Sanh hold out against the North Vietnamese?
But: How do Americans relate to the Vietnam environment?

[3] The U.S. 9th Division has intruded on a few isolated occasions. Not to be
confused with the ARVN 9th Division which has responsibility for Vinh Long
(the identical numbering is a coincidence), the U.S. 9th is based in Dong
Tam on the northern bank of the Mekong.
[4] A select few among the Viet Cong in the Delta have received training in
Hanoi. A select few among GVN officialdom in the Delta have received
training in the United States. (And France, too, but that's another story.)

(Similarly, a conclusion that because a year has passed since my last visit the material in this book is *out of date* misses the point of the whole exercise.)

I had still another reason for selecting the Delta. What people have in mind, I think, when they say "no more Vietnams" is a conflict that ties down a half million young Americans. But that is only one part of Vietnam. Another part is the complex military *and* civilian advisory and support system that exists in its purest form in the Delta. Already this system is functioning embryonically in many other countries, most notably in Latin America. It being understood that Vietnam is a special case — what country isn't? — it seems to me that, metaphorically speaking, in the Delta one can find in full bloom a plant which, although its shape and hue have been conditioned by the local environment, springs, nonetheless, from the same seed that we are carelessly scattering around the globe. On those grounds alone, the American effort in the Delta is worthy of examination.

Finally, there is the common criticism of a case study that it is not typical. One hears a lot of this in Vietnam: That project failed? Here we succeeded. That general is bad? This general is good. That battle was lost? This battle we won. I would argue that this study has no place in that debate. The essential matters under study here are the *criteria* for success and failure, which are uniform, and Vinh Long is nothing more than a context for examining these criteria.

The performance of the weakest (or strongest) professional football team may not be typical of quality, but it will be typical of how the game is played. This study focuses on how the game is played in Vietnam.

Contents

Introduction

"WE HAD TO DESTROY the town in order to save it." With these words, American officials explained why they had called for air strikes and artillery bombardments against provincial capitals in the Mekong Delta. The time was the Tet Offensive of February 1968. American bombs and shells were raining down on previously secure provincial towns in a determined effort to drive the Viet Cong back into the countryside. Though Americans were destroying the buildings that composed the Delta towns, they were confident the buildings would be rebuilt and the towns "saved." Whether the inhabitants felt themselves being "saved" by these bombardments was, of course, a question of perspective.

Vinh Long, the capital of Vinh Long province, was one of those towns. And now, through this fascinating study by Harvey Meyerson, we can see, as if peering down at magnified images in a microscope, how the American perspective on war and politics in Vietnam actually works and how it clashes with the perspectives that Vietnamese have on the same events. What we see is not presidents, cabinet officials, ambassadors, commanding generals, or other plenipotentiaries who give the orders and make knowing statements to the press. They are much too conspicuous to require high-powered microscopes to see. Instead, Meyerson focuses our attention on those Americans who must carry out the orders; those for whom a single province, like Vinh Long, is the whole world and the entire war.

In *Vinh Long*, we see for the first time at close range those previously anonymous young Americans who have been charged with "winning the hearts and minds of the people" and bringing the countryside under Saigon's "control." Theirs is a political war, a contest for hamlets and villages, a struggle between platoons and, at the most, battalions — all of them South Vietnamese. Remote to the Delta are the crushing, large-scale encounters between Hanoi's regulars and seasoned American divisions bristling with heavy firepower. Since Hanoi's troops have not penetrated that far south, the Delta people have been spared the devastation of these massive battles so typical to the northern provinces. But they know another kind of dread, one no less terrifying simply because it is less violent. And precisely because it is the scene of a more thoroughly political conflict than other regions of the country, Harvey Meyerson has chosen a Delta province to explain to us what the struggle in Vietnam is about.

Vinh Long is a compelling microcosm of the war because it so incisively yet sympathetically describes the cruel dilemma that young American officers — captains and majors, idealistic AID representatives only recently graduated from college — must face in an otherwise lush and productive land. The heart of the dilemma is that the village people doubt that the Saigon government is *their* government and virtually no act by these determined Americans can by itself change this opinion. They must advise, encourage, cajole, and sometimes threaten the Vietnamese provincial officials who are all there is of the Saigon government in a place like

Vinh Long. Yet so long as these officials are more concerned with their own survival and enrichment than with the political loyalty of the people in the countryside, the young Americans must desperately try to compensate for official neglect.

What sets *Vinh Long* apart from other books is that the broad American characterizations about the war are here examined against the merciless reality of the situation in a single province. If the "pacification" program is really effective in bringing the countryside under Saigon's "control," it should be effective in Vinh Long. If the breaking up of the Viet Cong into small units is really a sign that the enemy is falling apart, it should be clear in Vinh Long. What emerges from Harvey Meyerson's uncompromising scrutiny is not, therefore, a repetition of the old truths that the war is really a political conflict or that military force has limited effectiveness in preventing the Viet Cong from winning political commitment among villagers. Instead, his piercing journalist's eye reveals a new set of insights that make the conflicting purposes and perspectives of Americans and Vietnamese about the war stand out more sharply.

Through Meyerson's searching vision, we see that Americans and Vietnamese are operating in totally different organizational systems with entirely separate expectations and rewards. Saigon is trying desperately to maintain the framework of a national government including an administrative structure and a military chain of command. Yet so deep are the cleavages in Vietnamese society that all of Saigon's present and past leaders have been keenly aware that they must put discipline ahead of initiative if they are to preserve even the semblance of a government. While they certainly are not oblivious to the Viet Cong, these Saigon leaders often take the attitude that, under the circumstances, there is little they can do about them — as did the infamous General Thi who, as Meyerson reports, sat in his office in Sadec sipping tea while the Tet Offensive raged.

Naturally, Americans have been frustrated by such lack of initiative and indiscipline. But by trying to compensate for it, Meyerson shows, we have created a military advisory and "pacification" organization which has expectations that are not only beyond the capacity of Saigon to fulfill but are also not even closely related to the nature of the conflict. These expectations have grown out of the need to show "progress," especially during the one-year tours to which Americans' service in Vietnam has been limited. Meyerson deftly and devastatingly shows that by carefully selecting our criteria Americans have in fact been able to "prove that progress is definitely being made." The result is that statistics have had an almost hypnotic effect in determining our policies and in justifying the sacrifices our people have been making. Yet not even the Tet Offensive, which strikingly revealed how misleading our statistics could be, has shaken the faith of American officials in the need or validity of our statistical evidence of "progress."

In the aftermath of the Tet Offensive, I was left with so many doubts about the highly touted "progress" in the war that, in the spring of 1968, I decided to go to Vietnam to find out about the situation there for myself. Why was it, I asked, that in November 1967 the American Embassy in Saigon could report that 66 percent of the Vietnamese people were under Saigon's "control" and then just nine weeks later the Tet Offensive demonstrated that almost no area of the country was secure? In a report to the Foreign Affairs Committee of the House of Representatives on my study mission to Vietnam, I pointed out why the computer-tabulated reports on the percentages of the people under government "control" are so misleading. There are two general reasons: the first is that the reports are not even accurate assessments of Saigon's "control" because of the unwarranted interpretation of imprecise data; the second is that American officials have represented political "control" as being the same thing as political loyalty.

Among the specific reasons for the inaccurate assessments of Saigon's "control," I found three that are critical:

First, the basic data is gathered by United States officers who do not speak Vietnamese and whose approximately six-month tours as provincial advisers are so short that they cannot become familiar with the hamlets they are reporting on.

Secondly, of the eighteen criteria used to evaluate the security status of the 12,650 hamlets in Vietnam, only six relate to Viet Cong influence, and since all eighteen are given equal weight in the tabulation the other twelve can more than counterbalance unfavorable data.

Finally, the five categories, from A (the best) to E (the worst), by which the hamlets are ranked are rendered meaningless by the oversimplified interpretations of American officials. They have designated the A through C hamlets as "relatively secure" although this description is not even implied for all three categories, much less substantiated by the faulty information submitted from the field.

As Harvey Meyerson makes clear, this system works one of its greatest hardships on the young officers in provinces like Vinh Long. They know the fault of the system, yet they also know that if they try to challenge it their careers will be in jeopardy. As one young officer told me in May 1968, "Congressman, I work a 110-hour week. I downgraded four hamlets after the Tet Offensive and was immediately hit with a barrage of cables from Saigon demanding a full explanation for downgrading them. For the next couple of weeks I spent my time justifying the retrogression in those four hamlets. During that time I was not doing the things I should have been doing. I believe I am an honest man, and, although I hate to admit it, it may be a long time in hell before I downgrade another hamlet." This officer's dilemma is the dilemma of the men you will read about in *Vinh Long*. You will read of their anguish in a political conflict which few understand well even though many often recognize the unreality of our approach to it. And in the process you too will come to understand why our perspective on war and politics in Vietnam can lead us to believe that we will "save" Delta towns by destroying them as we did during the Tet Offensive.

If peace comes to Vietnam, it must come to Vinh Long. If you are to understand the prospects for peace, your chances are better if you understand them in Vinh Long. Everyone wants peace but not everyone can appreciate how nearly five years of American involvement have affected the prospects for peace. Though Harvey Meyerson has set himself the modest goal of explaining to us how the events in Vinh Long over the past two years have reflected American perspectives on the war, he has also succeeded in telling us a story about the human dilemma our young officers must face which will stick in our minds long after the facts of the days' news reports have drifted from our minds. What makes *Vinh Long* so important too is that Harvey Meyerson has told us something very perceptive about America and how we conduct ourselves in foreign lands. If there are "other Vietnams," will there be "other Vinh Longs"?

Congressman John V. Tunney

VINH LONG

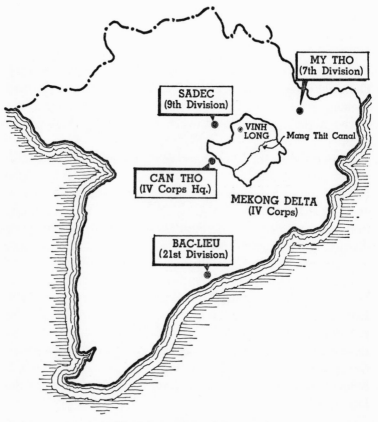

The Mekong Delta (IV Corps)

The Setting

VINH LONG PROVINCE is situated in the heart of the Mekong Delta on a large riparian island formed by the Bassac and Mekong rivers. Like most of the Delta, Vinh Long is flat — the highest point measures ten feet above high water level.

Among the sixteen provinces in IV Corps (which encompasses most of the Delta), Vinh Long ranks twelfth in size (1598.8 square kilometers), fourth in population (475,544), and first in population density. About 40,000 persons reside in the province capital, perhaps half that many in the seven district towns combined. The rest — at least 80 percent — are scattered over the countryside in 285 hamlets.

In fact, the hamlets *are* the countryside. Where one hamlet ends, another begins (as with American counties). Each hamlet consists of an amount of open rice paddy broken by patches of thick jungle. Hundreds of canals — some only rivulets, others as wide and deep as our rivers — run across the paddies and through the jungle. Most hamlet dwellers live in thatched huts scattered along the shaded banks of the larger canals.[1]

[1] See Appendix A for breakdown of GVN, American and Viet Cong forces in Vinh Long. The Viet Cong guerrilla organization is also discussed on pages 92–93.

PART ONE

The Mang Thit Pacification Campaign

The route to understanding in Vietnam leads from this proposition: The facts of any given situation are not always consistent with its reality.

Why?

Because in Vietnam, facts are like symbols in dreams. They mask certain fears and desires, the most frequent being fear of failure and desire for success.

VIETNAM brought to me a feeling of excitement. At first, I attributed this feeling to the presence of danger and the mysterious qualities of the Orient. Later, upon reflection, I added a third factor. Overlaying those mysterious qualities was something familiar. Yes, I had felt it on my arrival in New York after two years in Europe. There were these things: activity, a constant going and coming, the hammer of construction, variety, wealth, openness, optimism, and above all a mood that permeates the senses of constant change and rebirth. In sum, the Vietnam scene vibrated with that quality which can be called American dynamism.[1]

I reflected more. How did this wholesale transplantation of a way of living and believing influence the conduct of the war? Did it always act to our advantage? Will progress formulated in the spirit of American dynamism work in Vietnam? And the big question: If it works, will it reproduce? For our products are not built to last. Each new develop-

---

[1] The dispatches of other newly arrived correspondents seemed to confirm this impression. Their dominant theme was awe. The man-made deep-water ports, the jet airstrips, the modern bases carved in the wilderness, the constant flow of men and matériel worked with almost hypnotic effect. Here was American civilization advancing on the frontier.

ment comes out of a continuing process of obsolescence and renewal so pervasive and profound that we are not even conscious of it. For us to succeed in Vietnam with American methods we must generate an *indigenous desire for renewal.* If we don't, projects will burn out after they have run their natural course, at which point we will be required to regenerate momentum artificially with new projects. So it is not enough to look at a project in order to evaluate it. One must follow it over time and through the eyes of those individuals responsible for its evolution.

This is the story of a pacification project, how it was conceived and implemented and, most important, where it led. To get at an understanding of what was happening I have forsaken strict chronology and, by means of several case studies, have attempted to isolate those forces that influenced the project's eventual outcome.

I

An Idea Is Born

The briefing was conducted in the office of Deputy Ambassador William J. Porter at the United States Embassy in Saigon. Three economics officers did the talking. Porter, American director of the pacification program, and an aide listened and questioned. The theme was rice. At this date (July 27, 1966), South Vietnam, once a nation so rich in rice she helped feed the rest of Asia, had become dependent on rice imports to avoid famine. The turnaround began in February 1965 when the United States rushed in 25,000 tons.

Another emergency shipment arrived in August 1965. Since then, the flow of rice into South Vietnam had been continuous. It was expected to reach 850,000 tons in 1967.[2]

One of the briefers was standing before Porter's wall map tracing the principal rice transportation routes within South Vietnam when Porter's aide interrupted him to ask about an odd dogleg in the south-north route from the lower Delta — the nation's rice bowl — to Saigon. The rice flowed north to Can Tho on the Bassac River, then swung west almost to the Cambodian border, then doubled back down the Mekong River. Wasn't a more direct route available? One was . . . or rather had been, the briefer replied. Around the turn of the century the French had cut a canal northward from the Bassac to the Mang Thit River which flowed into the Mekong. The thirty-mile-long complex, known after its designing engineer as the Mang Thit–Nicolai waterway,[3] had served northbound rice barges until 1963 when Viet Cong occupied both banks of the Mang Thit and closed the waterway to traffic. The result was the dogleg remarked by the aide that added 2½ days' travel time for rice barges bound for Saigon.

Porter and the aide were intrigued. A few days later memos went out from the Deputy Ambassador's office to the economics section, inquiring about barge availability for rice transport from the lower Delta, and to the MACV office of General William Westmoreland for an opinion on the chances of reoccupying the banks of the Mang Thit. MACV responded coolly. Lieutenant General John Heintges, Westmoreland's deputy, advised Porter that ARVN lacked sufficient forces to secure the Mang Thit. Furthermore, the waterway formed the boundary between Vinh Long and Vinh Binh provinces and this presented a command problem.

[2] Actually, about 750,000 tons were imported in 1967.
[3] Hereinafter referred to as the Mang Thit.

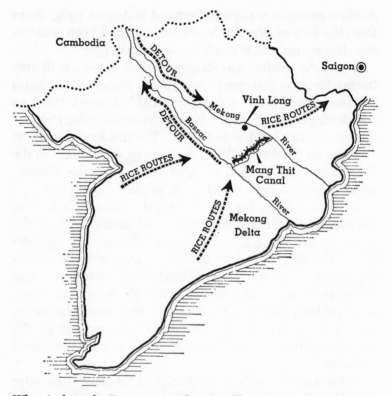

What Ambassador Porter saw: A dramatic "detour" in the rice shipment
route from the lower Delta to Saigon

By then, however, the Mang Thit idea had attracted the
sympathetic attention of Robert Komer, a member of the
White House national security staff with responsibility for
pacification. To keep the pot boiling, Komer took to sending
cablegrams to key Saigon offices — civilian and military —
inquiring as to the project's current status.

The Komer-Porter forces got a boost on November 1 with
the distribution through channels of a book-length report
(marked "Secret") dealing with *Some Economic Aspects of*

the Struggle in Vietnam. The report was the product of a government-sponsored on-the-scene study by Dr. Stephen Enke, a staff economist with that famous Santa Monica, California, "think-tank," the RAND Corporation. Enke closed his report with a number of recommendations. At the top of the list was a proposal to reopen the Mang Thit waterway.[4]

Distribution of the Enke report was followed almost immediately by an order from General Westmoreland's office to IV Corps headquarters. The Commander of United States forces in South Vietnam wanted his own report on rice flow with emphasis on military requirements. Fast! On November 14, it was on his desk. The report alluded to the Mang Thit project (which Westmoreland's order inquired about specifically) as "an important Revolutionary Development objective." Viet Cong controlled land along half the length of the waterway, the report said, but the area could be secured within six months with the assignment of about three ARVN battalions, six RF companies, one RF boat company, and an additional 1230 PF troops.[5]

[4] The relevant portion of the Enke report reads as follows:
"VC interdiction of Cross Delta waterway. In 1963, about 40 percent of the rice reaching Saigon from the Lower Delta was carried on the Mang Thit and Cho Lach canal system that connects the Bassac and the Mekong Rivers. There are now sufficient infestments of VC on both sides of this Cross Delta waterway to interdict it. As a result, such rice as moves from the Lower Delta to Saigon is mostly forced to move up the Bassac, almost to the Cambodia border, and then down the Mekong. This detour adds some 100 kilometers to the trip and exposes craft to strong currents on these rivers and longer exposure to possible VC attack. When rice-carrying craft from the Lower Delta are at the crossover point where they would leave the Bassac, if continuing to Saigon, they have a simple choice. Cambodia and world rice prices are 30 kilometers away. Saigon and import lowered prices are 175 kilometers away.
"The VC knew the importance of interdicting this canal. The USG [U.S. Government] knows the importance of clearing it again and keeping it secure. For some reason, the Province Chiefs of Vinh Long and Vinh Binh, which border these waterways on opposite sides, have not been able to agree and furnish the assets for a joint clearing operation."
[5] RF (Regional Forces) and PF (Popular Forces) are militia recruited at the province level.

The only way to pick up the troops Westmoreland's staff felt would be necessary to clear the canal was to get the Mang Thit designated a pacification area. Then troops would be diverted automatically to provide security for the pacification teams assigned to work in the hamlets. Tentative pacification plans for 1967, drawn up and submitted by each province, were then being processed in Saigon. Porter checked and found, to his chagrin, that the Vinh Long plan ignored the Mang Thit. The ranking American advisers in Vinh Long were quickly called in for a meeting with Vince Heyman, another Porter aide. Heyman made clear what Porter wanted. The stage was set for the climactic meeting on December 16 at Vinh Long province headquarters under the chairmanship of Major General Thang, national director of pacification.[6]

During the interim, the American provincial advisers had won over Colonel Diep, the Vinh Long Province Chief.[7] Diep presented a revised plan emphasizing the Mang Thit. Thang quickly resolved the last major stumbling block by assigning to Vinh Long two districts from adjacent Vinh Binh province, thereby placing both banks of the Mang Thit under Colonel Diep's jurisdiction.

The final revised campaign plan provided for assignment to the Mang Thit area of two ARVN battalions, four RF companies, eleven PF platoons, and three hamlet pacification teams. With the battalions providing primary security, eleven outposts would be constructed along the length of the

[6] The guest list included Brig. Gen. William Knowlton, Thang's American adviser; Maj. Gen. Manh, IV Corps Commander, and his co-advisers, Brig. Gen. William Desobry and Vince Heyman, the latter recently transferred to the Delta from Saigon; Brig. Gen. Thi, ARVN 9th Division Commander and *his* adviser, Col. Robert Bringham.

[7] Diep enjoyed a reputation as one of the Delta's more competent Province Chiefs. During the French Period, he was sent to the École de l'État Majeur in Paris. Early in the American Period he was sent to the Command and General Staff College in Fort Leavenworth, Kansas. He spoke fluent French, acceptable English, played tennis, and kept an excellent wine cellar.

canal in three six-week stages and manned by the newly recruited PF platoons. The RF companies would provide security for the hamlet pacification teams. By midyear — according to the plan — the canal would be open to commercial traffic. At that time American engineers would bring in a dredge to clear out silt pockets that might hinder deep-draft 500-ton rice barges.

After reviewing the new plan carefully, Westmoreland made it official. He advised Porter that he believed the canal could be pacified and ready for dredging by the first week in June.

In six months, then, GVN control would be restored in a strategic densely populated area, a key waterway would be reopened to civilian traffic, and eliminated would be a 2½ day detour and the Cambodia rice funnel. So pleased were Komer and Porter that the Mang Thit project (now known among Americans as "Komer's Kanal") was given status as the top priority pacification effort in the Delta.

The Objectives Considered

The Mang Thit project was conceived to meet two primary objectives:

1. Eliminate a 2½-day detour for rice barge traffic from the lower Delta to Saigon by reopening a waterway interdicted by the Viet Cong since 1963.
2. Halt the funneling of rice into Cambodia where prices were more attractive. (The detour took rice barges up near the Cambodian border.)

A secondary objective was pacification of the Mang Thit area.[8]

---

[8] Success in attaining the primary objectives was of course dependent on pacification. I list pacification as secondary because it was the belated dis-

The entire Cambodia diversion argument was based on this statement in the Enke report:

"When rice-carrying craft are at the crossover point when they would leave the Bassac if continuing to Saigon, they have a simple choice. Cambodia and world rice prices are thirty kilometers away. Saigon and import-lowered prices are 175 kilometers away." [9]

Enke offered no proof of rice diversion into Cambodia. No one had proof; I asked everywhere. The Cambodia funnel was a product of pure deductive reasoning.

But who was reasoning? And about whom?

An American economist was reasoning about Vietnamese. He was assuming Vietnamese would react like American entrepreneurs and immediately exploit the Cambodian "opportunity." I don't think we can make that assumption. The American merchant, tied to nothing but his own self-interest, would push across the Cambodian frontier, constructing roads, bridges, trading posts, etc. The Vietnamese merchant, on the other hand, is not so egocentric. He moves within different cultural boundaries. We can no more assume that the Vietnamese merchant would burst across the Cambodian border than we can assume that an ARVN field grade officer, after some education from us, would adopt American tactics, even those tactics that, seemingly, would improve his physical chances for survival.[10]

The other primary objective — to reduce the travel time to Saigon by 2½ days — was developed from equally dubious premises.

"Two and a half days," the American planners told me.

---

covery of the detour and the Cambodia funnel that led to the decision to pacify the area in the first place.

[9] One kilometer equals three-fifths of a mile.

[10] The problem of a rice spilloff into Cambodia resolved itself in 1967 when American economists prevailed upon GVN to increase the price to farmers. That ended the "temptation" exerted by Cambodia's higher prices. It is my argument, however, that the temptation existed primarily in the minds of Americans.

"Think of it!" The assumption being that Vietnamese shared our enthusiasm over saving 2½ days. But can we assume this? That is, can we assume the American concept of "time-saved" is accepted in a region steeped in a culture with a fundamentally different understanding of time?

As it turned out, Americans had a terrible time working up GVN enthusiasm over the prospect of saving 2½ days.

On June 6, 1967 — the project was now well under way — the IV Corps senior pacification adviser received a cable from Komer's office labeled "Action: Priority." [11]

"It is essential," the cable began, "that the impetus of the psychological advantage that has been gained from the recent operation on the Mang Thit Canal be maintained." The cable went on to request that the IV Corps senior adviser urge GVN to "explore the possibility" of sending a rice barge convoy up the canal.

So the adviser urged and GVN explored, and on July 15 a jubilant IV Corps pacification chief cabled Komer that GVN officials had held a big meeting and decided to send a thirty-barge convoy up the Mang Thit Canal! For good measure they would simultaneously dispatch a truck convoy up National Route 4. The whole performance had been designated "Economic Promotion Day," our man in IV Corps reported. The date would be set in the near future. The cable concluded,

"Official interest to your favorite project should finally get off the ground."

It never happened. No Economic Promotion Day, no barge convoy, no truck convoy, nothing.

I would submit that much of GVN's reluctance to act can be traced to a simple unintellectualized sentiment: Why all that effort to save 2½ days? After all: Before the Americans

---

[11] Porter left in May to become Ambassador to South Korea. Pacification was then integrated into the military effort under Westmoreland, and Komer was sent to Saigon as Westmoreland's deputy with responsibility for pacification.

"discovered" it, hadn't the Mang Thit been closed to traffic for four years without GVN showing much concern one way or the other? When the canal (which, remember, was conceived and engineered by Frenchmen) was available, Delta rice merchants used it. When it wasn't available, they went around it. At no time did they worry about it one way or the other.

The Mang Thit project would have made good sense in Kansas. In Vietnam it was a cultural anomaly. The specific misconceptions that directed American attention toward the Mang Thit are, to me, symptoms of a deeper malady.

The snobbery and sense of superiority of British and French colonialists, which often offends American sensibilities, insulates the British and French against errors we are so prone to make. The unabashed colonialists assumed their subjects to be inferior and therefore *different*. We assume our "associates" to be our equals and therefore (though we would never verbalize it this way) *just like us*. They aren't.

This genuine eagerness for friendship bubbles on the surface — we learn the languages, we fraternize with the people, we do all those things that haughty colonialists do not do. But beneath all the earthy involvement there flows an innate feeling of superiority guiltily repressed because it is so contrary to our better instincts. It is misleading, I think, to call this sense of superiority racism. Rather it stems from a faith in American techniques and a conviction, drawn from the American melting pot experience, that all peoples will accept those same techniques once exposed to them. They won't.

For reasons of their own, the Vietnamese *pretended* to accept American techniques, meanwhile going their own way. Time and again, as we shall see, Americans working on the

Mang Thit project showed themselves congenitally incapable of penetrating the Vietnamese shield.

Perhaps it was a refusal on our part. To do so — to accept the differences — would have amounted to an admission of failure in what we call "communication" but which is really not that at all. When an American aid worker says he is successfully "communicating" with the "people" of a foreign land, he means, most likely, that he is getting through with American techniques and ideas. Communication in this context is but a typically American mixture of salesmanship and the missionary ideal.

II

RD: Concept

The war in South Vietnam has accelerated the development of a new behavioral science called counterinsurgency. The objective of counterinsurgency is to defeat a guerrilla insurrection by a carefully apportioned mixture of military pressure on the enemy and social work among the population by educating them, enriching them, motivating them, and, finally, involving them in activities of the established government. In Vietnam this sort of thing is called "pacification."

Over the years, and especially since the ill-fated strategic hamlet program of 1962–63, South Vietnam has been transformed into a vast pacification laboratory. By 1965, Vinh Long province had scattered over its countryside a number of ten-man "Advanced Political Action" (APA) teams and forty-man "People's Action Teams" (PAT). In 1966, APA and PAT members were brought together to form the nucleus of several fifty-nine-man "Rural Reconstruction" teams.[12] Criteria for rendering a hamlet pacified were drawn up. Each team was to satisfy the criteria in a minimum of four hamlets per year — three months per hamlet. Cadre teams were encouraged to exceed the minimum. By midyear the program had degenerated into a paper exercise. Pacification teams moved in and out of hamlets like traveling salesmen. On their heels came evaluation teams from ARVN 9th Division. The evaluators would look around, formally pronounce a hamlet pacified, and move on. In this manner pacification proceeded at a phenomenal pace until the program's able national director, General Thang, after a few inspections of his own, concluded that the whole thing was ridiculous. He ordered all 1966 cadre teams back for one month retraining (initial training was three months) and came out with a more modest goal of two hamlets per team per year for 1967.[13] The 1967 program was introduced as "Revolutionary Development" (RD).[14] Without the sauce, RD consisted of the following:

Hamlets selected for pacification were divided into three categories according to priority. The top priority hamlet was

[12] Since GVN exercises control in the cities, pacification is concerned almost exclusively with the countryside.

[13] The American response to Thang's realism is revealing. A U.S. Government memorandum for field workers detailing the 1967 program carried this observation: "GVN has announced a planning goal of 800 hamlets and 1,000,000 people to be brought into the (pacification) program in 1967, but it should be possible to construct twice this number of hamlets."

That would have returned the program to the 1966 level which Thang diagnosed to be unworkable.

[14] The new name actually was a new translation. GVN kept the 1966 name which we translated in 1966 to mean "Rural Reconstruction." But for 1967, we decided to translate the same Vietnamese words as "Revolutionary Development." Since virtually no Vietnamese peasants speak English, the new translation evidently was intended for the inspiration of Americans.

This felt need to present a New Product, while urging field workers to push for the same goals that had wrecked the program the year before, betrays an unhealthy tendency to look first for an "image" of "progress" rather than an understanding of reality.

the *Ap Doi Moi* or "Real New Life Hamlet," which replaced the just plain "New Life Hamlet" of 1966. A hamlet selected for *Ap Doi Moi* status would be earmarked for several thousand dollars in local improvements — pigsties, fishponds, classrooms, footbridges, etc. The *Ap Doi Moi* would also benefit from the presence for six months of a fifty-nine-man RD cadre team.

The cadre belonged to the United States Central Intelligence Agency. The CIA paid their salaries and helped organize their training. All American cadre advisers at the province level were employees of the CIA.

The duties of a cadre team in an *Ap Doi Moi* were organized into ninety-seven "points" listed under eleven "criteria" arranged in descending order of importance. The key criteria were:

1. Eliminate the Viet Cong infrastructure.
2. Eliminate corrupt practices and discharge corrupt officials.
3. Develop a new spirit.
4. Establish popular government and social organization.
5. Organize the people for self-defense.

RD: Execution—Nga Ngay, a Mang Thit Ap Doi Moi

The Nga Ngay cadre team found their hamlet in comparatively good shape, physically. They had been preceded by an ARVN 9th Division "Civic Action" platoon. The platoon leader, an engineer, contrived a number of improvements — a new hamlet road, footbridges, attractive bamboo fences. Whether these structures were to become monuments to success or monuments to failure depended on the cadre team's ability to organize and motivate the population so that, when the six-month *Ap Doi Moi* program ended in Nga

Ngay, continuing GVN presence would be assured by popular involvement in continuing GVN programs. This was the crucial — determining — purpose of GVN's so-called Popular Associations to be established by the cadre in each pacified hamlet.

On July 17, 1967, I visited Nga Ngay with the intention of finding out how the Popular Associations were doing.

The Popular Associations had made no progress, for interesting reasons. A rice farmer said Nga Ngay had once before received favored status, during one of the interminable pacification programs, and that he had paid the 100 piastres membership fee in the then extant Farmers' Association. Shortly thereafter, the pacification program was abandoned, the Farmers' Association disbanded, and the Nga Ngay farmer found himself out 100 piastres. Another farmer said he had invested 600 piastres in an ill-fated cooperative launched as part of yet another pacification scheme. He never recovered the money. And so on. Nga Ngay residents stoically accepted the government-sponsored physical improvements. But they were not about to commit themselves to government-sponsored programs which — experience had taught them — had a way of collapsing at the hamlet dwellers' expense.

In the eyes of the American planners in Saigon these old programs were of course obsolete and to dwell on them was a sign of "defeatism." But the inhabitants of Nga Ngay, who did not rotate back to San Francisco, were not defeatists. They were simply realists.

ARVN support: Concept

A feature of the 1967 pacification effort was the unprecedented involvement of ARVN maneuver battalions in an elaborate military-support-of-RD program that looked absolutely beautiful on paper. ARVN would clear out organized Viet Cong resistance in an area selected for RD work. Then, as the cadre went about their assigned tasks, ARVN would help train provincial Regional Forces (RF) militia, who in turn would help train district Popular Forces (PF) militia, who in turn would complete the training of "Hamlet Self-Defense Forces," first established by the cadre as number five of their eleven criteria. Parallel to the army effort would be a police effort. Units of a newly created paramilitary National Police Force (NPFF) would work with ARVN until the area became reasonably secure, at which point National Police would absorb their functions.

For military purposes, RD was divided into three stages called "clearing" (destroying VC main force units), "securing" (cadre move in), and "developing" (long-range develpment programs take root). The three phases were programmed for completion within six months, at which time ARVN and cadre would move on, confident that the Viet Cong had been rooted out of that particular area for good.

The Revolutionary Development program assigned to ARVN a new role in society. It meant in effect a total break with the past. No longer could ARVN *take* from the people; instead they must *give* to the people. They had become part of a complex integrated effort. To get ARVN to grasp the full meaning of this radical change in their collective personality was a real challenge in depth psychology. But ARVN commanders and their U.S. advisers were up to the task. They prepared a special training course. Nothing was left out. ARVN troops were taught how to work with National Police and NPFF, how to initiate civic action projects, why they should not steal food from the people, how to make friends with the people, and so forth.

The training course was programmed for eleven and a half days . . . That should do it.

ARVN support: Execution—
The Case of 1st Bn., 16th Rgt.

The crucial "clearing" phase of the Mang Thit campaign was due to be launched the first week in January. Two ARVN battalions would saturate the area with sweeps, patrols, and ambushes, day and night; no important Viet Cong units would escape their net.

D-day came and went with no sign of ARVN. Weeks passed. U.S. advisers began making frantic inquiries.[15]

ARVN finally arrived in mid-February. As an expression of their concern over the delay, the two-week saturation campaign was cut to two days, whereupon the two ARVN battalions dug in and awaited the arrival of the cadre teams. Apparently the "make-friends-with-the-people" message had not yet penetrated the spirit of the two battalion commanders because each of them appropriated a hamlet schoolhouse for his command post and ordered the grounds covered with trenches.

On March 26, a multibattalion Viet Cong force attacked the base camp of one of the ARVN battalions: 1st Battalion, 16th Regiment, 9th ARVN Division. The Viet Cong were driven off with heavy losses (see p. 46 and following pages). A host of VIPs, including General Creighton Abrams, then Westmoreland's deputy, helicoptered to the scene to congratulate the victors.

Viet Cong probed at 1st Battalion several times thereafter

[15] The only unit to observe D-day belonged to the Viet Cong. Elements of the Viet Cong 306th Main Force Battalion, acting on intelligence (see pp. 93–96) arrived in Vinh Long on foot in early January. As it turned out, they had beat super-mobile ARVN to the scene by more than a month.

with no success. First Battalion was superb on defense. That turned out to be its problem. It was the RF and PF militia who had the primary defensive assignments. First Battalion was supposed to be hunting for Viet Cong, day and night. Four months after it arrived, 1st Battalion was transferred out at the urging of U.S. advisers who had become disenchanted with the unit's lack of aggressiveness. First Battalion's successors proved no better.

Left to their own devices, the RD support battalions assigned to the Mang Thit operated like huge stationary outposts, defending the ground on which they were encamped. The area was crawling with Viet Cong which the battalions bumped into occasionally, but they proved unable to mount any sustained effort that might keep the Viet Cong off balance. In military language, ARVN did not perform their mission.

U.S. Military Support: Concept

The anti-Viet Cong effort in Vinh Long province offered some of the qualities of a pageant. Units in a variety of garbs paraded through the countryside. To list the more noteworthy, with their American sponsors:

ARVN: MACV.
RF/PF: MACV.
RD Cadre: CIA.
Provincial Reconnaissance Unit (PRU): CIA "counter-terror" team.
National Police: U.S. Public Safety Division.
National Police Field Forces: U.S. Public Safety Division.
Armed Propaganda Team: USIA. Composed of Viet Cong deserters.

Into this galaxy of units were introduced, from time to time, new weapons and new techniques. Pressures from above were such that in almost every case the adviser was made to feel a degree of responsibility for the success of the innovation passed his way. He knew it was being implemented only after the most competitive lobbying within the upper reaches of the American establishment. He knew that its failure would reflect on the capacities of those who had lobbied on its behalf — his superiors. He knew that his superiors would be tempted to argue that the concept was sound and that therefore failure reflected on the capacities of the adviser in the field. Moreover, the adviser could not criticize his superiors without incurring their wrath and he could not criticize GVN without running the risk of disrupting "rapport," thereby bringing down the wrath of his superiors via another channel. So he pushed ahead blindly, taking the innovations as they came.

And they kept coming. For the parent agencies had grasped the elemental truth that one way of minimizing failure was to replace a dying program with a shiny new one. *That* was progress. Just find a fresh angle and push it!

The climate of competition among news correspondents — the pressures *they* felt from home offices demanding fresh angles — served the cause of the competing government agencies. Correspondents were led from one new project to another. Each gimmick had its hour of glory in the press. The reader may recall them: "tunnel rats," "Riverine force," "starlight scopes," the "sniffer." Something *new* was always happening in Vietnam.

Each of these projects was a product of brilliant minds. Each was grounded in logic and conceived with lucidity. Each was transplanted in Vietnam with logic and lucidity intact. Completely intact.

U.S. Military Support: Execution—
"Taking the night away . . ."

May 9, 1967. Dusk . . . The by-invitation-only audience included the ranking GVN military and civilian officials in Vinh Long and their American advisers. They had been brought together for the unveiling of a dramatic new contribution to the war effort — an invisible beam that would, as the saying goes, "take the night away from the VC."

They were gathered in a park along the riverfront around two shiny jeeps each mounting what appeared to be a standard searchlight. An American second lieutenant in his early twenties paced nervously alongside the jeeps, alternately muttering over some note cards and barking orders of mysterious nature to a sergeant working a shortwave radio in one of the jeeps.

At a sign from the Senior MACV adviser, the lieutenant cleared his throat violently.

"Okay," he shouted, still pacing. "Gentlemen, you have here two M-151 A1 jeeps and you have mounted on these jeeps two 23-inch Zenon short arc searchlights with rated candlepower capabilities of 75 million. And with, I might add, an overdrive up to 125 million." He stopped and glowered out at the now silent crowd gathered around him in the darkness, while a Vietnamese translated.

"Okay . . . Now the power source for the searchlight itself is a heavy duty generator rectifier that puts out 180 amps — 24 volts." Translation. The lieutenant pacing.

"Okay . . . Now these lights have a rated range of 3000 meters for infrared and 8000 meters for invisible light." Translation.

"Okay . . . Now each light has 6400 mils capability and an elevation of 900 mils." Translation. Muttering from the crowd. Inscrutable smiles.

"Okay . . . Now, oh I forgot . . . I mean, what I mean is, this is a searchlight *section*. It has" — racing now — "one section chief, an E5, three crewmen, two infrared binos, two medoscopes, and one M60 machine gun." Translation.

"Okay . . ."

I stopped taking notes and repaired to a riverfront stand for a bottle of soda. There I recognized a half dozen Vietnamese officials who had drifted over from the ceremony. It was a typical Delta evening — heavy and quiet and, because we were near the river, thick with mosquitoes. I squatted on the quay and sipped at the soda. Shiny black water slapped softly against the quay. To my left, a light appeared on the river. A marker? No, it was moving, approaching ever so slowly. It was a sampan. Eventually, as I watched, the sampan drew abreast. Someone in shorts moved across the light. Then back again. The sampan did not rock, it glided, mysteriously, as if it were an organic extension of the river. Maybe it was. Maybe it always had been, maybe . . .

I wasn't conscious how long it took the sampan to pass out of sight. Five minutes, perhaps ten, fifteen . . . I don't know. I began to feel uncomfortable from squatting and walked back toward the crowd.

An American major filled me in. Some problem, he said. U.S. Navy PBR boat. Out there in the river. Somewhere. Planned for infrared searchlight to focus on it. Turn night into day. But can't locate "goddam boat." Oh it's out there. They've got radio contact.

The lieutenant, sweating profusely, was conversing with his radio operator. The low tone of voice meant to disguise his anxiety only intensified it. "What's the matter with those bastards!"

The lieutenant was holding the mike now, desperately trying to get a reading that he could coordinate with the supersensitive dials on his searchlights.

It was no use. They never found the goddam PBR boat.

The performance was salvaged by the searchlight unit's infrared binoculars. Looking through them, it was possible to pierce the darkness all the way to the opposite bank. The binoculars were circulated among the crowd with happy results.

I got hold of a pair and gazed at the opposite bank for a few seconds. As I brought the glasses down, I caught the eye of a Vietnamese captain standing nearby. He was smiling. I wondered how many dozens of such devices he had seen come and go.

"Look!" I said with mock seriousness, "I spotted a VC on the other bank."

He walked over and took the binoculars.

"Ah yes," he said after a moment. "You are right. I see him now. He is standing on the bank. I think he is, how do you say? — I think he is pissing." [16]

When confronted with such tales, U.S. officials are apt to say, "Better to have tried and lost than not to have . . ." Or, "Anyone can criticize, what we need are more positive programs." The trouble is that out of this optimism constantly renewed on the American side came a cynicism constantly renewed on the Vietnamese side.

---

[16] The Americans were at first captivated by this extraordinary discovery dispatched to their care from the Great Laboratory.

But the super-searchlights could go only where jeeps could go and where jeeps went was rarely where the Viet Cong went. After a while the Americans stopped talking about the searchlights.

III

Communicating "Progress"

> *Hamlet:* Do you see yonder cloud that's almost
> in shape of a camel?
> *Polonius:* By the mass, and 'tis like a camel, indeed.
> *Hamlet:* Methinks it is like a weasel.
> *Polonius:* It is backed like a weasel.
> *Hamlet:* Or like a whale?
> *Polonius:* Very like a whale.

Americans in Vietnam are engaged in a split-level exercise in communication — with Vietnamese and with other Americans. Communication between levels is complicated inasmuch as Vietnamese share certain values outside our experience. With regard to pacification, the difficulty is compounded by the psychological nature of the American goal. We want to win a people's hearts and minds. For success, we must penetrate the Vietnamese psyche; we must understand exactly what it is the people desire.

The means we have selected for reaching our goal is "progress," a nebulous concept in the Vietnamese setting. Progress is communicated across cultures and up the chain of command by means of a number of rituals, the most highly developed of them being the briefing.

During my stay in Vinh Long, Ap Bay hamlet — the "showcase" Mang Thit *Ap Doi Moi* — received a seemingly endless stream of American dignitaries: generals, congressmen, cabinet officials, foreign aid officials. They came by helicopter over what was known locally as the "VIP run":

Saigon–Ap Bay (nonstop fifty-five minutes) or, more frequently, Saigon–Can Tho–Ap Bay. In the latter instance, the visitors would travel to Brigadier General Desobry's IV Corps headquarters in Can Tho, take in a briefing on how well the war was going . . . drinks, lunch, and a trip into the "field." The theme was, "But don't take our word for it. Look for yourselves. Why we've got a project under way in a Viet Cong heartland and you'd be amazed . . ."

Let us reflect for a moment on the dress and manners of the Can Tho visitor as General Desobry leads him to the awaiting helicopter for the trip to Ap Bay hamlet. Quite possibly he is a man of subcabinet rank — an Assistant Secretary of State or Defense — though you wouldn't know it to look at him. For if he is like most visitors he will have followed the advice of his hosts and donned army fatigues. This stripping of civilian garb is the first act in an experience that bears cumulative effect on the visitor's powers of judgment. He begins to feel that others — they call him "sir," but, he can sense it, they consider him a softie — are measuring him.

Now an accompanying officer suggests he take an inside seat in the helicopter. ("It's safer.") A young door gunner sees him fumbling, and helps latch his safety belt. The pilots twist dials, they are laughing (at what?), their voices are lost in the roar. The machine lifts, banks, accelerates . . . The visitor rubs his damp palms on his fatigues and looks out over the jungle and the rice paddies. The Washington conference rooms where he confidently presided — they seem so far away . . .

Now the helicopter approaches Ap Bay hamlet.

Up there in the sky, strapped in, turning, descending, the door gunners pointing .30-caliber machine guns at that distant tree line . . . enemy territory . . . the helicopter

doorway wide open . . . naked . . . the little knot of men
in the clearing beneath . . . the helicopter dropping faster
. . . the jungle rushing up . . .

And suddenly you are there, the helicopter is gone, and
you are bouncing along this dirt road in a jeep and the American officer in the front seat has just released the safety on his
carbine. It takes a truly strong-willed man not to become
possessed by a powerful desire to perform coolly.

All this works subtly on a visitor's confidence and therefore
on his independence. Should he meet the challenge without
a noticeable slip, there will follow a rush of relief which can
become inflated like this:

> To himself: *"I passed the test!"*
> To others: *"We've got the VC on the run!"*

If, however, the visitor gets by the shift in environment
with his critical faculties intact, he will then find the road to
reality blocked by a much more formidable hurdle — the
briefing itself.

On July 15, 1967, a member of the White House staff was
outfitted in fatigues and helicoptered to the Mang Thit campaign headquarters. There he was seated on a bench before
the Province Chief and a battery of multicolored charts. The
Province Chief reported 12 classrooms built, 4 classrooms repaired, 86 small bridges built, 12,000 meters of secondary
road repaired, 1200 meters of main road surfaced with
crushed rock, 2 hamlet offices built, 1 market 70 percent completed. While the building was going on, ARVN killed 395
Viet Cong, the Province Chief said, and captured 15 Viet
Cong, 2 heavy machine guns, 2 light machine guns, 5 BARs,
7 submachine guns, 2 B-40 rocket launchers, 4 M-1 rifles, 106
grenades, 100 steel saw blades, 1 generator, 2 communications systems, 1 PRC10 radio, 8 claymore mines; and ARVN

destroyed 1 grenade factory, 10 Viet Cong information houses, and 190 grenade traps. Meanwhile, GVN had won the hearts and minds of 13,084 of the 30,760 peasants living along the banks of the Mang Thit, plus 777 others who had migrated to the Mang Thit from Viet Cong areas further inland.

Next came the "walk-through." The theme was, "But don't take my word for it. Walk through the hamlet. See for yourself." Maternity-dispensary? Brand new, right here. Pigpens? You see them. Freshly stocked fishponds? Vegetable demonstration plots? Hamlet self-defense force? New road? New bridges? They are all there.

Indeed, by American standards the *Ap Doi Moi* hamlet of Ap Bay underwent steady improvement between February 1967 when a pacification cadre team arrived, and late July 1967 when the cadre team left. We find it hard to believe that a hamlet with a *new* road, *new* bridges, *new* dispensary, *new* classrooms, *new* fishpond, *new* pigpens, has *not* progressed. But what about the hamlet dwellers? The briefing is structured on the assumption that they too were impressed.

GVN officials, who knew better, found it in their interest to keep quiet. They knew that the bulk of the peasantry acceded to government by day and Viet Cong by night. They had learned to live with that stalemate. It was not uncomfortable. In order to ensure its continued existence, however, they were obliged to convince the Americans that the stalemate was not a stalemate at all but a progressive shift in GVN's favor. Fortunately, the Americans had a weakness for measuring progress. GVN exploited this weakness by embracing it. They adopted American values and American tools of measurement and applied them to their own purposes.

Witness the walk-through. On briefing day a representa-

tive of the Province Chief made sure that cadre were
distributed through the hamlet so the visitor would encounter them at every turn, purposefully going about their appointed tasks. The so-called hamlet self-defense force (a
paper organization in Ap Bay) was rounded up and put to
work on its training patch near the new hamlet road. Others
were ordered to man the new pigpens. If the visitor was of
special importance, school kids were lined up along the road
and told to wave and smile and sing at the visitors. It's true.
I watched the preparations more than once. The picture Ap
Bay presented to visitors was about as close to reality as a
stage play prepared by a propaganda ministry.

The adopted procedure thus made it virtually impossible
for visitors to judge at first hand the highest priority pacification project in the Delta. Between the visitors and reality
stood the props and language of the briefing.

The real situation was something else. According to that
July 1967 briefing, the Ap Bay cadre team — on the scene
almost six months — had completed 90 percent of its eleven
"criteria" and ninety-seven "points," thus rendering the hamlet "secure" from Viet Cong. What the briefing did not report was that the cadre who at this point were supposed
to be living among the people were actually spending their
nights huddled in a fortified outpost. They reported the
hamlet secure, but they sure didn't act like it was secure.
They had reason. Viet Cong penetrated the hamlet at will.
On July 17, two days after the briefing described above, Viet
Cong blew up a wall and part of the roof of Ap Bay's new
maternity-dispensary and kidnapped two masons hired to
build it. The building was of course feverishly repaired in
time for the next walk-through.

The fact is that when the cadre pulled out in late July and
an archway was posted over the new hamlet road with an

inscription pronouncing Ap Bay a secure *Ap Doi Moi* hamlet, the hamlet was no more secure than it had been before the cadre arrived. The people were loyal to the government during the day; they were loyal to the Viet Cong at night.[17]

IV

Ap Tan Thang and Ap Tan Qui

On August 26, 1966, "Rural Reconstruction" cadre teams were sent to Ap Tan Thang and Ap Tan Qui, adjoining hamlets on the Mang Thit, and two RF Companies were brought in for security — an impressive total GVN force of almost three hundred men, or one-fifth the combined population in the two hamlets. Physical achievement was immediate and immediately recorded on the progress charts. But the Vinh Long hamlet program was then running behind schedule, so, less than a month later, on September 23, an ARVN 9th Division inspection team declared the two hamlets pacified. On the morning of September 25, cadre and RF were withdrawn. That night Viet Cong dismantled seventeen foot-

[17] It is often said that popular loyalty to the Viet Cong is forced. Perhaps. But GVN's pursuit of loyalty seems even more open to question. An example:

RD funds were set aside to pay men from Ap Bay for helping on the construction of three new outposts near the hamlet. This was a sensible way of involving the local population in a GVN project. Private inquiries in Ap Bay and at the construction sites revealed, however, that the workers were not being paid. It seems that the cadre were working both sides of the street. First, they diverted the funds for salaries to their own pockets. Then they came around to each inhabitant and said: Pay us 1000 piastres or we will be obliged to conscript you for outpost construction. The men working on the outposts were those who couldn't afford the bribe.

There was quite a bit of this sort of thing.

bridges constructed by the cadre. The next morning the hamlet chief elected under the cadre's auspices fled for his life.

The American cadre adviser had objected to the withdrawal, and through his efforts new cadre teams were assigned to Ap Tan Qui and Ap Tan Thang. Thereafter, the hamlets became that American's pet project. He got them designated *Ap Doi Moi* for 1967.

A pocket battle now began for the loyalty of the population in the two hamlets. On the GVN side were numbers and firepower, unlimited resources, two handpicked cadre teams, and the personal attention of a highly competent American cadre adviser. The Viet Cong responded with stealth and steady pressure.

When the cadre left on a Tet holiday, Viet Cong agents grenaded the homes of three families who had sheltered them.

On March 17, cadre and RF in Ap Tan Qui beat off an attacking Viet Cong force; five Viet Cong bodies were recovered, other enemy dead and wounded probably were carried away. In this kind of war, it amounted to a major GVN victory.

But the Viet Cong did not let up. In April each member of Ap Tan Qui's newly organized hamlet self-defense force received a handwritten warning signed by the Viet Cong district secretary. Despite subsequent tightening of hamlet security, five defense force members were kidnapped on June 5.

Then, on the night of June 15, the Viet Cong got the kind of break they were looking for. A Viet Cong sniper shot the Ap Tan Thang cadre team leader in the neck. His subordinates radioed for a Vietnamese Air Force (VNAF) medical evacuation helicopter. VNAF refused the request. They were reluctant to go in at night. Next the cadre radioed the

Mang Thit campaign headquarters at the Caumoy Bridge —
just two miles downstream from Ap Tan Thang — and
asked for help from the Vietnamese River Assault Group
(RAG) unit stationed there. The RAG refused. They would
not move their powerfully armed river craft off the dock
until morning. Two hours were thus spent in futile pleading.
As the hamlet dwellers looked on, the desperate cadre
finally loaded their now unconscious chief into a tiny sampan
and struck out on their own for the Caumoy Bridge. He died
en route.

The meaning of this sorry GVN response to the plight of a
loyal servant was not lost on the local population. All remaining hope for saving Ap Tan Thang and Ap Tan Qui was
snuffed out a month later when the American cadre adviser,
his tour completed, rotated home. Understandably, his re-
placement did not feel the same emotional involvement with
the two hamlets. He had other ideas, probably no less laudable. The cadre teams were withdrawn and Ap Tan Thang
and Ap Tan Qui lapsed into their former state.

But progress continued! All that happened was that Ap
Tan Thang and Ap Tan Qui were replaced on the progress
charts by new favorite hamlets of a new generation of advisers.

V

Meanwhile . . .

In April 1967 the target date for opening the Mang Thit canal
was moved back two months to early August. On August 8, in
ceremonies at the project site presided over by Premier Ky
himself, the Mang Thit Canal was formally declared "pacified." Many of those in attendance found it difficult to follow
Ky's dedication speech. ARVN troops had made contact
with Viet Cong less than a mile from the speaker's platform.
The din from dive bombers and artillery was tremendous.

The canal, of course, was anything but pacified. The ceremony on August 8 honored an illusion. The situation along
the canal was deteriorating. A secret reevaluation concluded
that the canal would not be ready for interprovince traffic
before November or December.

Came December. The truth no longer could be avoided.
The Vinh Long advisory team's report for that month
contains the following entries:

> The people of the Mang Thit Pacification Campaign
> Area remain for the most part neutral . . . The cadre
> have been less than successful completing criteria I and
> II in this campaign area; the VC infrastructure is still
> largely in place and an unacceptable amount of local
> corruption remains . . .

Now the report for January 1968 (prepared before the Tet
attacks):

Recession of the Mang Thit Campaign 1967 pacification hamlets to nightly Viet Cong control is a very real possibility during the first quarter of calendar year 1968 . . . The Viet Cong secret government remains in place . . . The only elements presently preventing recession to full night time VC control are the two ARVN battalions screening the Special Zone and these are scheduled to move on or about 8 February to new positions . . . It will then be extremely problematical whether the remaining territorial forces can enforce night security . . .

After a year of dynamic existence, the first priority pacification project in the Mekong Delta had not yet reached first base. The most optimistic members of the Vinh Long team still hoped rice merchants from the lower Delta might be induced to ship the February harvest to Saigon via the Mang Thit. These hopes were dashed — conveniently — by the Tet attacks. Traffic on the Mang Thit halted altogether. Six months after our so-called Tet "victory" the situation remained at a standstill.

VI

Conclusion

I know of no people who have established schools so
numerous and efficacious, places of public worship better
suited to the wants of the inhabitants, or roads kept
in better repair . . . The American makes associations to give entertainments, to found seminaries, to
build inns, to construct churches, to diffuse books, to
send missionaries to the antipodes; they found in this
manner hospitals, prisons, and schools . . .
ALEXIS DE TOCQUEVILLE (1830)

The Vietnam debate has a way of losing itself in a maze of
policy considerations: Should we have backed Ho Chi Minh
in 1945? Should we have backed Diem in 1955? Should we
have escalated in 1965? Should we stop the bombing? If
the bombing is stopped, can it be started again? If it is
started again, should it be escalated to include the docks at
Haiphong? If it is escalated to Haiphong, what response can
we expect from the Soviets? From the Chinese? From the
French? From the Yippies . . . ?

Policy considerations certainly are important, but they bear
little relevance outside this context: What is happening in
Vietnam? (Or: How is it that so much concentrated grit and
power and wealth is not producing results?) To go after that
question is to reach for the roots of the Vietnam problem.
More, it is to diagnose those forces that have conditioned the
American response to revolutionary change, a response keyed
to *open* involvement accomplished by "participation." I
would suggest that the answer is in those insights into the

American character put forward by De Tocqueville so long ago.

The Vietnam experience represents to me a prodigious attempt to transplant America's magical mix in a foreign culture and make it grow. Mentally, the Americans in Vietnam are still in America. They build, they tear down, they build again, they compete with one another, and almost everyone assumes that *by promoting his own personal advancement he is contributing to the general welfare.*

The result of this highly competitive approach is a proliferation of programs, each either run jointly by competing agencies or run by one agency in competition with programs run by other agencies. Information radiates out from the countryside through a system resistant to American central control.

I could see it happening. During the planning stages, those concerned with the Mang Thit project shared a common picture of what was about to occur. As the project got going, however, the picture broke up. It did not blur or shatter. Instead it multiplied. Each participant developed a point of view which served his interests and/or the interests of his agency. Obtaining a picture of the Mang Thit project from Saigon was like looking down a shifting kaleidoscope.

The different pictures merged again after it was all over. But by then nobody cared. Attention was focused on new projects.

The rotation process — twelve months in Vietnam for the military, eighteen months for civilians — has the effect of preventing Americans over there from understanding just what they are doing. Each new generation arrives filled with enthusiasm: "Well maybe *they* couldn't pacify a hamlet in three months. But *we* can." In this climate, there is nothing to be acquired from study of past experience but dangerous "defeatism."

Thus, life takes on a bizarre rhythm always a beat away from reality. By the time the failure of any project becomes apparent, its implementers have been sent home to America, and the new team, not wishing to dwell on the past, is moving forward with that year's new program. Reality becomes a thing of tomorrow, always tomorrow.

What is apparent at any given moment as progress, then, is not progress but part of a process of constant self-rejuvenation within the American establishment. Since any new program can be expected to generate an initial élan, the focus assures an image of constant success. It is as if one chose to record the impact of the charge of the Light Brigade by focusing on rank after advancing rank of gallant cavalrymen, while ignoring the carnage.

Meanwhile, on the other side of the camera, taking it all in, are those whose hearts and minds we are after. To the Americans, Vietnam is a counterinsurgency laboratory, alive with new projects and new ideas. But to the people in the hamlets, Vietnam is a counterinsurgency graveyard overgrown with weeds and speckled with monuments: abandoned model settlements, forts, refugee camps. Needless to say, the mood of the graveyard is not the same as the mood of the laboratory.

In sum, as I watched the Mang Thit project unfold I became convinced that what was occurring was an unsuccessful transplant. We were trying to inject that suffering people with the American dream and they were rejecting it as the bloodstream might reject a foreign body.

And so, a year later, there it was — the Mang Thit project — a once shiny American automobile, abandoned and rusting in a roadless jungle.

"Experts"

During my stay in Vietnam and in the course of subsequent research I often consulted experts, namely *technicians* (having a specialized knowledge in a technique, such as precision bombing or plant defoliation), and *area specialists* (students of the culture and politics of a region, Southeast Asia for instance). I found their knowledgeability and calm assurance comforting. At first. The more I consulted them, however, the more I became conscious of an uneasiness beneath the calm. The uneasiness rippled gently as conversation moved out of the Vietnam context into a global context. Gone now were those healthy disagreements among the experts over the conduct of the war (to bomb or not to bomb, to support Thieu or Ky, to pacify or pulverize). Now, in a special way, the Vietnam experts were united in fear. The fear was not explicitly stated, nor did it drive them to extreme positions. What it did was to work subtly on their judgment.

Among area specialists the fear emerges out of a kind of *Asia-centeredness*. ("It is time to recognize Asia's true importance" is a common refrain.) For better or for worse, the Vietnam war has succeeded in focusing American attention on Asia. The fear is that this new attention will give way to a

new revulsion if the Vietnam experience proves disillusioning.
A humanistic domino theory.

"What worries me most," writes Professor Edwin O. Reischauer, one of our most compassionate and enlightened Asia
specialists, "is the effect that our withdrawal from Vietnam
might have on ourselves." He predicts that a less than honor-
able U.S. settlement in Vietnam could lead to "grass roots"
disenchantment with Asia fueled by a "sophisticated neo-
isolationism" defended on grounds that "after all East is East
and West is West." [18]

Reischauer's fear that we will turn away from Asia is exag-
gerated to the degree that he is preoccupied with Asia; that
is, his emotional center of gravity is not in the United States
but somewhere midway between the United States and Asia.
Because of this, although he is eminently qualified to explain Asia, his judgment on United States *national interest* in
Asia must be weighed against his own *emotional and intel-
lectual interest* in Asia.

Another characteristic of the Asia area specialist is a tendency to exaggerate the global impact of events in Vietnam.
After observing that precipitous withdrawal would mean
"welching on commitments not just solemnly made but repeated," Reischauer concludes, "One wonders what effect
this might have in other countries, such as Japan and *our
European allies* [italics added] that have been relying on
commitments made by us." [19]

As one who arrived in Europe in 1965 as we were beginning our troop buildup in Vietnam and spent the next year
and a half reporting on the commonly unsuccessful efforts of
Rusk, McNamara, and Ball to wring from our NATO allies

[18] Edwin O. Reischauer, *Beyond Vietnam: The United States and Asia*
(New York, 1967), pp. 14–15.
[19] *Ibid.*, p. 14.

some sort of commitment to the "common struggle" in Southeast Asia, as one who watched Gaullism (including its offshoots) feed and flourish on the Vietnam issue, I found Reischauer's observation a little hard to swallow. Again, it seems that Professor Reischauer is blinded to the true nature of European reaction to the United States commitment in Southeast Asia by his own emotional commitment to the people and cultures of Asia. The essential humanism which is his strength as a scholar is his weakness when it comes to evaluating United States national interest.

It is interesting, and revealing I think, how one of our most enlightened area specialists and one of our most enlightened technicians, who are sharply at odds over means, come together in their interpretation of Vietnam's world repercussions. General Maxwell D. Taylor might be citing Professor Reischauer when he writes,

"I am certainly deeply convinced that such a disaster (U.S. pullout "not imposed by a superior enemy") would propel a shock wave of dismay which would spread rapidly from the epicenter in South Vietnam, extending around the globe, which would effect every international relation we have and every alliance, *including NATO* [italics added]."

And again:

"They [our allies] would raise the inevitable question, 'Can we count on the Americans any more anywhere? Why rely on them in Europe if they are not trustworthy in Asia?' " [20]

Taylor's error is in his approach which is that of the *strategist-as-statesman.* He measures the reactions of our allies as he would the reaction of allied armies strung across a broad front and backed up by the army of the United States. The

[20] Maxwell D. Taylor, *Responsibility and Response* (New York, 1967), pp. 21–22.

trouble is that nations do not always react like armies, especially when they do not perceive a direct threat.

Taylor's error has, I think, another dimension to it. Like
Reischauer, though for different reasons, Taylor feels personally involved. In his case it has to do with tactics. Taylor's
response to the so-called "threat" of so-called "wars of national liberation" was to espouse a doctrine of "limited war."
In Vietnam, Taylor's doctrine is being put to the test. That
word again. One hears so much from government officials
about Vietnam being a test. For Taylor, the word has an
added shade of meaning. Not only is Vietnam a test of *our*
commitment and *our* will, but it has become a test of *his* military doctrine.

It is important to make the point clear. Experts often are
criticized as "inhuman calculators," "talking IBM machines."
That's not true! The expert is a living breathing human
being with passions, fears, obsessions, joys, ambitions — and
with a great deal of scientific material at his disposal. How
he disposes of this material is not determined by the immut-
able laws of science. It is determined by those highly
charged inconstant impulses that govern human motivation.

Men committed as Taylor and Reischauer are committed
can contribute to our understanding of Southeast Asia. But
they are not the best men to judge United States interests in
Southeast Asia, no matter how expert their knowledge, no
matter how deep their appreciation of the "true importance"
of Asia. For their recommendations tend to reflect an intel-
lectual conflict of interest that can be just as compelling as
any economic conflict of interest.

PART TWO

The Battle on Easter Sunday

No South Vietnamese military operation of any consequence is launched in IV Corps — the Delta — without American advisers joining in the planning and execution, offering suggestions at every level and calling in support when necessary.

The advisers are everywhere. At IV Corps headquarters in Can Tho, each ARVN staff officer is assigned an American "counterpart." A U.S. advisory team is attached to each of the three ARVN division commands and to each of the thirty-two ARVN battalions in the field. Each province staff is "paralleled" in all its functions by members of a U.S. "Sector" advisory team. A "subsector" advisory team lives in each provincial district.

American combat support comes mainly from the air. American helicopters ferry troops and lay down a fire base. American jets strafe and bomb. American PBR boats patrol major waterways. Specially equipped American C-47s light the night with flares and tracers from their Gatling guns.

In military terminology, all this is known as the American advisory and support role. It occupies four thousand Americans in IV Corps.

I

March 23, 1967

IN HIS five months in the Delta Bob Graham has never seen mist so thick. It seems to steam up through the jungle matting. Though his watch reads only 6:00 A.M. he feels hot and clammy. And nervous. The battalion will break camp in a half-hour. They will march south for six kilometers through swampy jungle, then dig in on the edge of a Viet Cong base area. The mist cuts visibility to a few feet.

Graham begins to feel Responsible. Hal Meeker calls this Graham's big weakness. "It eats away at him," Meeker says. "He thinks that if something happens to one of us he'll be to blame. Of course we're only four guys, and we're really in their hands and this worries me too sometimes, like when everyone starts yelling in Vietnamese."

Captains Harold Meeker and Robert Graham, and Sergeants J. D. Atkins and Raymon Spivey make up the American advisory team attached to 1st Battalion, 16th Regiment, 9th ARVN Division. For six weeks now, the battalion has been operating along the Mang Thit–Nicolai Canal in Vinh Long province. Their mission is to provide security during the construction of outposts, and to protect hamlet pacification teams as they move in stages down the thirty-mile canal.

Bob Graham commands the advisory team. He is also its youngest member (twenty-five); the only one with a college education (Providence College, 1963), the only one from a big city (New York), and he looks the least like a Hollywood soldier: a little overweight with a face a little too round and

a habit of speaking a little too excitedly. Graham is acutely
conscious of his inexperience and his deficiencies in the John
Wayne department. He compensates by trying all the
harder to *act* like a commander. He worries constantly, pub-
licly, and with eloquence about his men, sometimes to their
embarrassment; he growls over the radio at the slightest
delay in supplies or support. At Sector headquarters in Vinh
Long city, people say Graham thinks his is the only unit in
the Delta. And that's what Major Andrew Palenchar likes
about him. Palenchar is Graham's immediate superior, adviser to the 16th Regiment headquarters unit stationed at the
Caumoy Bridge, 4½ miles downstream from 1st Battalion.

As the battalion departs on foot at 6:30 A.M. the mist
begins to lift, carrying off some of the weight of Graham's
Responsibility. The Vietnamese soldiers wave goodbye to
their wives and children who live with them in the field and
who will follow in a few hours by boat. Everyone seems relaxed, and why not? Six weeks on the notorious Mang Thit
Canal and nothing worse than a few mines, grenade traps,
and a little sniper fire. No one has seen a Viet Cong, dead or
alive.

The first indication that all might not be the same at the
new position comes in the dense undergrowth a few hundred
meters below Caumoy Bridge. There they discover a bunker
reinforced with concrete. In the Delta, where the fighting
ebbs and flows through the jungled villages and the rice paddies, concrete positions are a rarity (excluding government
outposts). When a concrete bunker turns up it means the
Viet Cong have been present in force for a long time and that
they enjoy the acquiescence if not the support of the surrounding population; or, that they *are* the surrounding population — men, women, and children.

Beyond the bunker the now wary marchers detect many
more signs of Viet Cong presence. foxholes, thick mud firing

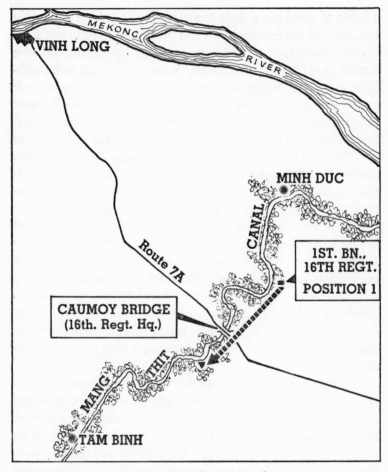

1st Battalion's line of march

walls along the canal, and a hut piled with bales of razor-sharp punji stakes.

Shortly after 10:00 A.M., the battalion reaches its plotted position. Neither Graham nor Captain Duc is pleased with what he finds. The flat terrain is unusually dense, woven through with coconut, banana, and mangrove trees, bamboo grasses six feet high, and an assortment of thick shrubs. Crisscrossing through the jungle are dozens of little feeder canals up to four feet deep and twenty feet wide.

Duc and Graham plot a roughly triangular perimeter enclosing a land mass of about seventy acres. The Mang Thit forms the base. The very tip of the triangle breaks out of the jungle onto a rice paddy, 700 meters inland. Second and 3rd Companies' positions run along canals about fifteen feet wide. Thick jungle closes around the banks of these canals and, in the case of 1st Company, around the positions themselves.

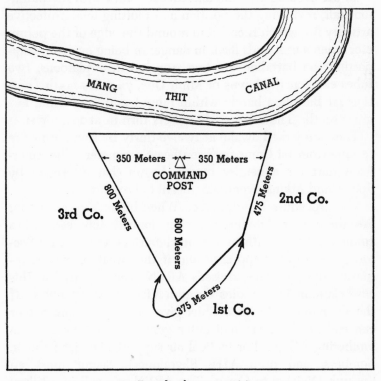

1st Battalion's new position

The defenders set to work immediately, digging trenches and hacking out fields of fire. Some cut trees for single-log "monkey" bridges across the feeder canals. Vietnamese navigate the slippery logs with dexterity; Americans dread them. To get from the command post, at the center of the seventy-acre position, to 2nd Company's perimeter means traversing 300 meters of jungle and a half dozen monkey bridges. Graham begins to have visions of himself stumbling through the jungle at night, tripping over roots and shrubs, falling off monkey bridges, covered with mud, bullets crackling, mortars exploding, a cacophony of foreign gibberish . . .

In the evening Graham and Meeker work with the battalion staff, reviewing the position and plotting final protective artillery fire which is called in around the edge of the perimeter when a unit finds itself in danger of being overrun. Supporting the battalion are two .105 howitzer platoons, two tubes each, at the towns of Minh Duc, 7½ miles north (putting 1st Battalion barely within range) and Tam Binh, five miles south. The exhausted advisers turn in at 11:00 P.M.

They are jerked awake at twelve-thirty by small arms fire coming from 1st Company's southeast perimeter. The Americans dart for a nearby trench, begun that afternoon by Spivey and Atkins, eventually meant to be a bunker.

The procedure is automatic. When his unit comes under fire the senior American adviser immediately establishes communications with higher headquarters, in this case Sector, gives a quick appraisal and if the situation merits, requests support. The adviser's ARVN "counterpart," in this case Captain Duc, radios through Vietnamese channels. If the Vietnamese Province Chief gives the green light, Sector can call in American helicopter gunships or "Spooky," the lumbering AC-47. For tactical air support (i.e., jet fighters, bombers, and prop A1H. Skyraiders), Sector must go through Division to Corps. The ARVN can call in artillery on their own, since it's their own artillery, and additional ARVN troops. But if they want to heli-lift the troops — and they often do — an American "parallel" is required.

Graham has barely radioed his report of incoming fire when it stops. In the sudden silence, Duc and Graham make for 1st Company. Halfway there, a grenade explodes with a dull whump, then another. Small arms open up, followed by short bursts from 1st Company's .30-caliber machine guns. But by the time Graham and Duc arrive on the line, all is quiet again.

Graham observes one ARVN dead in his trench from a bullet in the head and another wounded from grenade fragments. About ten meters out from the trench line a Vietnamese wearing only black shorts lies face down and still.

Duc gets the story and passes it on to Graham in the pidgin Vietnamese-French-English they use to communicate. During the initial bursts of incoming fire, when the defenders instinctively ducked, two Viet Cong crawled toward 1st Company. On signal the firing stopped and one of the infiltrators leaped up and hurled two grenades before he was cut down. The other, this time using the grenades as cover, managed to make off with 1st Platoon's radio. It seems the platoon leader had retreated from his slightly forward position when the firing started.

March 24 . . .

First Battalion intelligence receives reports that numbers of Viet Cong have been observed filtering through hamlets to the south and east of their position.

At about 11:00 P.M., 2nd Company is probed with small arms and automatic weapons fire. No casualties.

Saturday evening, March 25, Easter Eve . . .

First Battalion's positions are in pretty good shape. Fields of fire have been cleared up to sixty meters and strung with twin double aprons of barbed wire. The outer reaches are planted with grenade traps, trip flares, and claymore mines. As night falls the defenders send out squad-size ambushes and hang little kerosene lanterns on the barbed wire. The slightest pressure on the wire causes the lanterns to rock, a good way to detect infiltrators.

At the battalion command post the advisers sip beer and make plans for Easter. Intelligence continues to report Viet Cong movement and as Sergeant Spivey points out, the VC have on successive nights probed first one side of the perimeter, then the other. But defenses are good and a full moon is rising; the Viet Cong rarely operate in bright moonlight.

Shortly after 9:00 P.M. someone or something touches off a grenade trap in the jungle opposite 2nd Company. Duc and Graham go to check. It is dead quiet. Moonlight silhouettes the soldiers poised along the entrenched line. Rifle muzzles point across the stark no-man's-land to the blurred jungle fifty meters off. There the flickering lanterns hang still as if suspended in the hot humid Delta air.

Duc completes a hushed voice interrogation of the company commander and issues his orders. Whump! Whump! Whump! — up go the illumination flares from 1st Battalion's .60-mm. mortars. The flares explode overhead like giant Roman candles; under their eerie incandescent glow, a patrol moves out from the trenches, across the open ground, until, one by one, they disappear into the jungle.

They find nothing.

Next, Duc calls in his ambushes and orders the area saturated by the Tam Binh battery. Walking back to the command post, as the ground shudders from the incoming .105s, Graham tries his pidgin again.

"You think VC?"

"Yes," replies Duc. "Beaucoup." He places the battalion on 100 percent alert.

II

One of the weird paradoxes of guerrilla warfare is the way men sweat, fight, and die in little pockets in the countryside, while all around them life goes on as usual. At the Province Chief's residence in Vinh Long city — only a few miles from entrenched 1st Battalion — strings of carnival lights hang over the grounds and the air is filled with the gay sounds of Vietnamese folk music and hearty conversation. The ranking Vietnamese and American officials in Vinh Long province are assembled at a lawn party for a popular departing U.S. civilian aid worker. After a sumptuous Vietnamese repast, the carnival lights are dimmed and a deputy province chief presents home movies taken during his recent State Department-sponsored visit to the United States — Beverly Hills, Detroit, New York, Albuquerque . . .

Out near the edge of the crowd the voice of the narrator mixes with the harsh crackling of a radio. The noise comes from a low concrete structure with a gaping double-hinged doorway. Inside can be seen several desks, a wall map speckled with pins, and a few men in olive fatigues, among them an American major who is nibbling on sliced turkey apparently brought over from the party. This is the province

TOC (Tactical Operations Center). The TOC maintains radio contact with units in the field. The major is Robert Chaudrue, the ranking night duty officer.

The party breaks up toward midnight. The American officers, in white shirts and ties, led by Lieutenant Colonel Theodore Roth, senior Sector adviser, stop off at the TOC to see how things are going. Chaudrue can report only a light probing of 1st Battalion, 16th Regiment. "Let's hope it stays quiet," Roth says.

The visitors have scarcely left when the radio begins to jam slightly. It sounds like natural interference. Chaudrue notes this in his log, takes off his boots and fatigue shirt and stretches out on a cot. The radio operator sits hunched in the circle of lamplight by the crackling machine, reading a pocket book.

꒰

Lying on his back in the darkness, Spivey squints at the luminous dial. Almost midnight. He sits up and swings his legs off the cot and scratches his bare chest under the dogtags. Boy is it hot. He looks around. He looks at the three other figures on cots, at the tarpaulin sagging over them, at the jungle closing around them . . . Christ! Spivey pushes away the mosquito netting and puts on his boots, pants, and fatigue shirt. He stretches out again and lights a cigarette. A few yards away, Atkins lies on his back, smoking too.

"What's the matter, Sarge?" Graham whispers. "Can't you sleep?"

"I don't know, sir, just grabbing a smoke."

"I can't sleep either," Graham says.

The heavy damp stillness is broken by a distant pinging noise.

"Sounds like a round." It's Meeker's voice.

"Nah," says Spivey, "probably a bird." And louder: "So everyone's awake."

Grunts all around.

"Mind if I turn on the transistor?" Meeker asks.

More grunts.

A mindless conversation develops, backgrounded by rock and roll from the Armed Forces Network.

At about 1:00 A.M. the conversation is interrupted by two sharp rifle reports. Seconds later, all hell breaks loose — machine guns, mortars, small arms, grenades, from every direction, as if suddenly they have been dropped into the middle of an exploding ammunition dump. The four advisers roll out and crawl toward the unroofed bunker, Graham dragging the radio. They are followed into the hole by a tumble of Vietnamese.

"Is anyone hit?" "Is anyone hit?" "No." "No." "I'm okay." "Who?" "Meeker." "Where's the radio?" "Jesus." "*Where's the radio?*" "Get him the radio!" "Where is it?" "Goddam Vietnamese landed on it." "Where? Where?" "Right here, right here." Graham grabs the mike and pushes the talk button. "What's the matter?" "I don't know." "Call Sector." "It's not working." "What's the matter?" "I don't know dammit . . . Oh Christ the cord . . . He broke the cord!" Atkins goes for the other handset, returns. "Able Lakes four five, this is Muggy Stages one one, over. Able Lakes four five, this is Muggy Stages one one, over. Four five, four five, this is one one, over." "What's the matter?" "What's going on?" "I don't know, they're not answering." "Oh Jesus . . ."

⚓

Young Captain Blaine Hendricks likes listening to radio messages, even radio static. He got that way after being assigned as adviser to Cai Son training center for local militia, five miles west of Tam Binh. Nothing could be duller. So he spends his evenings on a cot by the radio pretending he is out there with a battalion or a subsector team.

On Easter Eve Hendricks is pursuing his fantasies when Graham comes up on the radio, calling Sector. As Hendricks listens idly, the 16th Regiment adviser at Caumoy Bridge, Major Palenchar, intercepts Graham and asks what is going on. "We're under heavy attack, we need support quick," Graham says. "Hold it . . . wait one," Palenchar says. A pause, then, "We're under attack too." Palenchar starts calling Sector. Just then Hendricks hears the distant thump of what he guesses to be mortars. It can't be the Caumoy Bridge or 1st Battalion, they are out of hearing. Now comes the radio call sign of Major Earl Gutschinritter, leader of the Tam Binh Subsector advisory team. Gutschinritter is calling Sector. But no one can get through. Apparently the VC have jammed Sector's frequency.

Hendricks radios 9th ARVN Division TOC in Sadec, fourteen miles west of Vinh Long city. Using Hendricks as a relay, Division restores communications by getting everyone to switch from Sector to Division frequency. It all takes less than five minutes. But if Hendricks hadn't been listening, it might have taken precious minutes longer.

"We are being mortared." It is Gutschinritter's voice. Major Chaudrue takes the mike from his radio operator.

"Are you under direct attack?" Chaudrue asks.

"No, just mortars and recoilless, I think. About forty rounds so far."

Chaudrue quickly parallels a request for Spooky to support Gutschinritter in Tam Binh; a Spooky already is en route toward 1st Battalion. Then Chaudrue calls Sector and routs out Colonel Roth. By the time Roth and Colonel Diep, the Province Chief, arrive at the TOC the situation is like this:

Mortars are raining on Tam Binh district town. At the Caumoy Bridge, seven miles to the Northwest, the 16th Regiment command post is being harassed by small arms and mortars. And, in the middle, 1st Battalion stands under heavy attack.

Roth and Diep conclude that 1st Battalion is the prime target and that the mortar barrage is meant to silence Tam Binh's artillery which already is booming away in support of 1st Battalion. For further support, Roth and Diep request helicopter gunships and the 3/2 Cav.

The 3rd troop of 9th Division's 2nd Armored Cavalry Regiment is bivouacked just west of Vinh Long city. Its fifteen armored personnel carriers and 160 men offer tremendous firepower — nine .50-caliber machine guns, thirty-one .30-caliber machine guns, three .81-mm. mortars, two .57-mm. recoilless rifles.

Both requests are granted. The Cav will take Route 7 thirteen miles southeast to the Caumoy Bridge, then swing due south to 1st Battalion. Roth and Diep decide to ride with the Cav as far as the bridge where they will link up with Palenchar at the 16th Regiment CP. But Diep grows impatient waiting for the Cav to mount up. Despite the danger of an ambush, he collects an armored car and a company of regional militia and, with Roth, takes off down the road. A few minutes later the 3/2 Cav's armored vehicles rumble through the sleeping province capital and turn onto Route 7. It is 1:00 A.M.

"Spooky five two, Spooky five two, this is Able Lakes four five, over . . ."

"Four five, this is five two, over . . ."

"This is four five. ARVN battalion under attack by unknown number Victor Charlie. Coordinates x-ray sierra two two four three zero seven, repeat x-ray sierra two two four three zero seven. Did you copy, over . . ."

"Four five, five two. Roger copy. Out."

Air Force Captain Monte Montgomery banks his AC–47 out of its lazy orbit and proceeds almost due east. He has been on CAP only a few minutes. CAP: Cover Air Patrol. Daily from dusk to dawn at least one AC–47 flare and gunship called "Spooky" circles 3500 feet above Binh Thuy airfield outside Can Tho. It can be dispatched to any of the hundreds of lonely Delta outposts vulnerable to Viet Cong attack.

Montgomery has no trouble spotting 1st Battalion: A half-mile-square area alive with flickering lights from muzzle flashes and tracers — more concentrated fire than he has ever seen.

"Muggy stages one one, this is Spooky five two, over . . ."

"Spooky! Spooky!" Graham yells over to Duc. The commander waves jubilantly. No American weapon is more popular among the Vietnamese than Spooky. The bullets from its Gatling guns roar down from the sky in a molten red stream, 600 rounds per second. The two-million-candle-power flares turn the night into day. The effect is exhilarating. Vietnamese defenders have been shot trying to get a better view of the performance.

Graham marks the battalion command post with a flare, radios the distances to the perimeter, and Spooky goes to work.

But the Viet Cong continue to press the attack. Here at the command post, several hundred yards in from the besieged flanks, rifles, machine guns, grenades blend into one continuous vibrating roar.

At 1:30 A.M., the command post loses radio contact with 3rd Company. Meeker and Spivey take up position on either side of the bunker facing the jungle between them and 3rd Company. Flares light up the tangled screaming undergrowth, it seems full of shadows.

Graham waves off Spooky and Duc calls for final protective fire.

A runner reports: 3rd Company commander requests permission to fall back twenty meters; the Viet Cong have turned his left flank near the canal. Permission denied. Duc orders a relief party forward from headquarters company. He puts the battalion executive officer in charge. Meeker and Spivey join the party. The Americans ignore the monkey bridges en route to 3rd Company and splash through the slimy waist-deep canals. A handful of Viet Cong have infiltrated around a .30-caliber machine gun position near the Mang Thit bank. They drive back the infiltrators and regroup around the machine gun.

One of the two men assigned to the weapon lies dead in the trench. The reliefers have barely caught their balance when, after jabbering excitedly on the radio, the executive officer leads them in a pell-mell dash back toward the CP. They leave behind two men and a BAR to help the beleaguered machine gunner.

"What's going on?" yells Meeker as he and Spivey jam ammo clips and grenades into their fatigues. "I think they have broken through 2nd Company," Graham says.

The reliefers take off again, tripping and thrashing

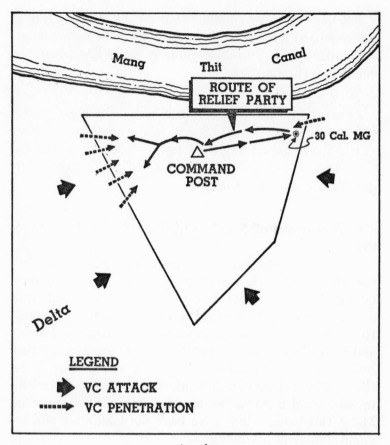

Attack

through the thick undergrowth. About fifty meters from the
2nd Company line, they encounter a half dozen retreating
defenders. A Viet Cong grenade assault has carried through
at an isolated point near the right flank. Once again the reliefers form for assault, and moving forward, crouching, firing, reloading, moving forward . . . they succeed in regain-
ing the trench line, just in time to help beat off an enemy

charge, then another. Each charge was a large-scale repeat
of the attack on 1st Company two days earlier — intense fire,
little men in black shorts crawling forward, leaping up,
screaming, hurling grenades.

By now, Graham and Duc have developed a pattern.
When the enemy charges, Duc calls in artillery. When the
enemy pulls back, Graham calls in Spooky. The helicopter
gunships requested by Sector arrive, but Graham refuses to
put them on target. The Viet Cong are using .30- and .50-
caliber machine guns, Graham says. The helicopters would
be sitting ducks.

It is now almost 3:00 A.M., two hours till daylight. Can
the battalion hold out? Graham believes Yes, if they can just
get a little more firepower . . . Duc is thinking the same.
"Mai Bai . . . Mai Bai . . ." he shouts to Graham.

Mai Bai is Vietnamese for airplane.

Three A.M., *Easter Sunday*

The Viet Cong prefer to be dispersed and hidden by daybreak. Thus the attackers might be expected to break contact at any moment. Brigadier General Lam-Quang Thi, the
youthful (thirty-six) 9th ARVN Division commander, his
senior staff officers, and their American advisers stand before
a wall map in the Division TOC and ponder the usual problem: How to guess the Viet Cong avenue of retreat?

Ninth Division intelligence reports that elements of the
Viet Cong 306th main force battalion have been sighted re-
cently around Hoa Binh Village, only three miles south of 1st
Battalion. Excellent canal routes lead from Hoa Binh to 1st
Battalion. Moreover, radio reports indicate that the mortars
bombarding Tam Binh are positioned somewhere in Hoa

Binh Village. A Viet Cong retreat to Hoa Binh seems likely. The plan begins to jell.

Hoa Binh is shaped like a y lying on its side, the tail flowing west into the Mang Thit opposite Tam Binh district town.[1] The 2/2 armored cavalry troop bivouacked on the Bassac River (not to be confused with the already moving 3/2 Cav) will proceed thirteen miles northeast to Tam Binh. Third Battalion of the 16th Regiment and the 1st of the 14th will be heli-lifted to the two eastern tips of the y. Everyone will converge.

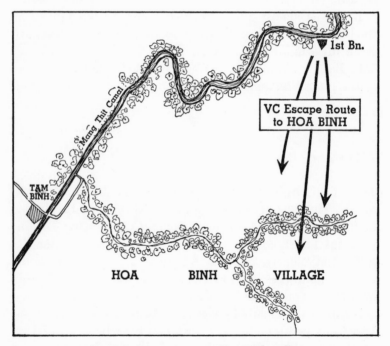

The Viet Cong retreat to Hoa Binh Village

[1] Delta villages tend to follow the serpentine contours of Delta canals. The thick jungle along the canals eventually gives way to open rice paddies, forming a silhouette that the military call a "tree line."

The 2nd of the 16th and the 43rd Ranger Battalion will act as reserves, to be committed in the event of heavy contact. The Caumoy Bridge is selected as Division field command post. The whole operation is code-named Long Phi 999. Will it work? It should . . . The Delta is flat as a board, the terrain is 75 percent open rice paddy, the government controls the air and enjoys overwhelming fire superiority on the ground. And yet:

How many times have ARVN officers and their American advisers stood like those of 9th Division, before wall maps studying the bewildering lacework of canals leading away from a given position? How many times have the officers concluded "Here!" and mounted massive reaction operations — artillery, jets, helicopters, troops galore — that end without sighting a single enemy? The Viet Cong are masterful escape artists. And yet:

What else can a hulking division do? The orders go out:

To 3rd Battalion, bivouacked just outside Sadec: Prepare to be convoyed to Vinh Long airfield for 7:00 A.M. liftoff.

To 2nd Battalion in Cao Lanh, fourteen miles northwest of Sadec: Move up to 3rd Battalion's bivouac and stand by.

To 43rd Rangers, providing security for the abuilding My An Special Forces camp, seventeen miles northeast of Sadec: Prepare for early morning liftoff.

To 1st of the 14th, encamped thirty-eight miles southeast of Sadec: prepare for early morning liftoff.

Helicopters: Major Jim O'Neill, U.S. Army Aviation liaison officer assigned permanently to 9th Division, guarantees fourteen transport ships (called "slicks") with gunship escorts. A C&C (Command and Control) helicopter outfitted with multiple radios will overfly the operation from beginning to end, offering General Thi and his staff a clear view of and direct radio contact with the units in the field.

Artillery: A .105 platoon will move by road to the Caumoy

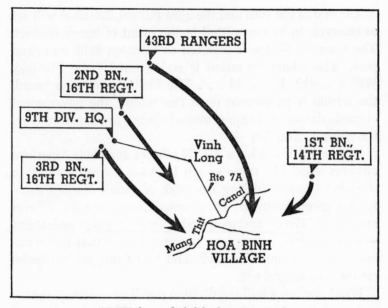

ARVN forces heli-lifted to Hoa Binh

CP. The besieged Tam Binh platoon will be resupplied at daybreak by heavy duty Chinook helicopter. (Under the Viet Cong mortar barrage, densely structured Tam Binh had literally caught fire. But the howitzer platoon there had not panicked, they had not even employed counter battery fire against the mortars. Instead, they had pumped rounds at a furious rate into the jungle around 1st Battalion — 800 shells during the crucial hours between 1:00 and 3:00 A.M.)

Tactical Air Support: More complicated. Normally, a Delta air strike comes after a laborious weeding-out process, starting at the province level and working up through Division and Corps to TACC, Tactical Air Control Center in Saigon. TACC dispatches airplanes all over South Vietnam.

Lieutenant Colonel John Nichols, U.S. Air Force liaison officer to 9th Division, does all right on his requests. He obtains quick approval for air cover for the division reaction force, as well as immediate support for 1st Battalion. In anticipation of the latter, Nichols scrambles a little single engine Cessna (Radio Call sign: "Bart 92"), one of nine U.S. Forward Air Controllers (FAC) scattered over the 9th Division area of operations. The FAC's job is to hover over target and guide in fighters and bombers.

"Muggy stages one one this is Bart nine two, over . . ."
"Bart nine two, this is one one, over . . ."
"This is nine two. I have Skyraiders five minutes out, over . . ."

Graham and Atkins move to a 1st Company forward bunker pointing onto the rice paddy — better view. Graham has the FAC work the Skyraiders along the flanks and along the tree line 300 meters opposite him across the open paddy.

The prop Skyraiders are followed in short order by two flights (two planes to a flight) of F-100 jets out of Saigon's Ton Son Nhut airfield. Meeker and Spivey, who have been helping along the perimeter, tumble into the bunker with Graham and Atkins to watch the show. But each time the jets come screaming through the blackness, their .20-mm. cannon pile-driving shells into the earth, the advisers flatten: Instinct will permit nothing else.

Back at the CP, Graham reports the Viet Cong fire seems to be slackening. Of course anything would seem quiet after the jets. But it is 4:30 A.M., and the Viet Cong have to withdraw before daybreak. Withdraw? Why, that's true . . .

Graham begins to vomit. The Vietnamese house boy offers a cup of tea. Graham sips the tea and resumes his duties on the radio. The fire *is* slackening.

III

General Thi and his American adviser, Colonel Robert Bringham, reach the 9th Division heli-pad just as the Command and Control helicopter, their flying command post, drifts down out of the sky, its rotor blades kicking up a little whirlwind. The Vietnamese general and the American colonel clamber aboard, and in an instant the pad is quiet again.

They head southeast. Major William Meehan, commander of Vinh Long's 175th "Outlaws" helicopter company, is at the controls. Their radio call sign: "Outlaw Six."

Already, other specially equipped helicopters are converging on target:

From Soctrang airfield, Major James Eberwine, 657 Medical Company commander, and his medevac crew. Call sign: "Dustoff."

From Vinh Long airfield, staging area for the troop lifts, Major Robert Millward, Outlaw maintenance officer, and his flying repair shop, complete with mechanics and spare parts. Call sign: "Roadrunner."

From Can Tho, riding out to watch the show, Colonel Jack Dempsey and Major Don Casper, commanding officer and operations officer, 13th Army Aviation Battalion, embracing all helicopter units in the Delta. Call sign: "Delta Six."

All this is standard procedure for any operation. The Command and Control (C&C) ship orbits at 1500 feet and lower, Roadrunner at 2000, and Dustoff at 2500. When Delta Six shows up, he is assigned an orbit by the mission commander.

Also on hand, as usual, are two bouncy Cessnas — the Air Force FAC who will guide in air strikes, and the Army "Shotgun" who buzzes around adjusting artillery and looking for signs of Viet Cong. Earlier that morning, Shotgun had called in gunships after spotting Viet Cong in sampans exfiltrating from the 1st Battalion area. But the Viet Cong had picked a canal crowded with families on their way to market and had mingled with them — to borrow a phrase — like fish in water. The gunships had no choice but to withhold fire.

Now, however, Hoa Binh Village shows no signs of life. Nothing extraordinary about that. Some peasants have a nose for sandstorms or typhoons. The Delta peasant has developed a nose for air-ground operations. A few orbiting helicopters and spotter planes are enough to send him scurrying for the family bunker made from packed mud that graces a corner of nearly every quaint thatched hut in the Delta.

The debarkation point for the first lift, designated LZ (Landing Zone) Alpha, is an open rice paddy facing south into an east-west tree line 300 yards thick, the top branch of the *y*. As with hundreds of previous heli-lifts, the plan calls for the troops to leap out of the helicopters into the paddy mud and slosh their way to the tree line to hunt for the elusive enemy.

As the C&C ship orbits in view, LZ Alpha is "prepped" by two flights of Skyraiders. They appear out of nowhere, drop eight 250-pound bombs into the jungle, and disappear. A helicopter "gunship" platoon, hovering nearby, is ordered to reconnoiter the tree line. They buzz over at treetop level, pronounce it clear, and head off to collect their charges, the fourteen loaded troop transport helicopters ("slicks") closing on a "reporting point" two miles west of Hoa Binh.

The approaching slicks carry an ARVN company, plus two American advisers, Captain Tom Mitchell and Sergeant Carl Bolin, the latter an easygoing Louisianan who this morning

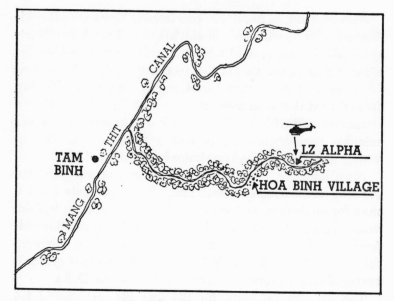

LZ Alpha: The first troop lift

finds himself full of wonder and incredulity. He had joined
the battalion two days earlier and this is his first operation in
Vietnam:

"There I am pretending I'm asleep — couldn't sleep; little
nervous, I guess — and Captain Mitchell shakes me and says
'We're moving out.' 'To where?' I say, and he says 'To Vinh
Long,' like we go there every morning at four o'clock. So
down we go to Vinh Long in a convoy, pitch dark, and Lieutenant Latham and Captain Mitchell line up everyone along
the runway in little bunches of ten — 'sticks' they call them
— for the helicopters. They keep saying 'Oh another hot
walk in the sun' like they do *that* every morning too. The
helicopters lift up and sweep around and land, one next to
each stick, and we get in and take off. I'm thinking 'these
helicopters are flying awful close together' . . . But then I

become interested in the terrain. It looks so pretty and peaceful. After a bit those gunships meet us and we begin our descent. I see a lot of water buffalo and pigs running around but no people. I think we'll all get off the aircraft and get in one of those beautiful tactical formations and go right in. The gunships start putting in rockets to cover us. They sound pretty devastating. I think 'boy, if there's anything in that tree line' . . . Then, about ten feet off the ground our door gunners open up and I realize we're taking fire . . ."

Surprise is total. Aware that "negative suppression unless fired upon" are the door gunners' orders, Captain Lon Paul has just shouted into the intercom, "Why the hell are you . . ." when what is probably a B-40 rocket impacts just in front, splashing mud over the windshield and causing his co-pilot, Carson Snow, to feel his heart suddenly stop and drop away, and then come back thumping like crazy. Two ships back, Tom McCarthy turns to see why *his* door gunner is firing and in that instant there comes a bright flash; plexiglass splatters through the cockpit. A ricocheting bullet crashes into the helmet of co-pilot Vance Shearer, nineteen. He bounces against the control panel, his hand still gripping the cyclic stick. The helicopter begins to tip over on its side. McCarthy fights to right it.

Outlaw frequency erupts: "Receiving fire . . . receiving fire . . . receiving fire . . ."

Back comes Major Meehan: "Outlaws get out of there!"

Bullets thud against the helicopters. ARVN soldiers tumble into the paddy mud. Like a swarm of bees, the flight of helicopters seems to rock slightly, then swings forward, up, and out of LZ Alpha.

All but one. It sits there, the spinning rotary becoming visible, spinning slower, slower, till it stops.

•

"This is Outlaw one seven. I'm down in the LZ. I'm down in the LZ. I can't get out. This is Outlaw one seven . . ."

Twenty-five hundred feet overhead, Major Eberwine pushes his medical evacuation ship into a whirling descent. It's automatic.

"Dustoff coming in."

"We've got you."

The gunships approach from east to west, pouring rockets into the tree line, Dustoff right behind. At the last moment, Eberwine banks sharply and drops into LZ Alpha alongside Outlaw 17. He reports, "This is Dustoff. Receiving fire . . ."

From the air, antlike figures can be seen moving between the two ships. Time passes. They are taking too long.

"Dustoff, this is Outlaw Six [Meehan]. You'd better get out of there."

"This is Dustoff. We're still loading . . ."

"Come on out Dust . . ."

Finally: "This is Dustoff. I'm coming out."

The ship inches forward along the ground. From its radio come the words "Oh my God . . ." And Dustoff explodes in a ball of flame.

Two ships on the ground. No radio contact. Not with the helicopters, not with the troops of 3rd Battalion. What is going on down there?

"This is Delta Six. I'm going in after the next air strike."

Meehan advises against it. Colonel Dempsey acknowledges the transmission without comment. Two F-100s appear out of the sun and strafe the tree line and disappear again. Major Charlie Gordon, the Outlaws' gunship platoon leader (Call sign: Maverick Lead), goes in from the west at 250 feet to reconnoiter. All is quiet. He banks 180 degrees and comes back along the tree line at 200 feet. Still quiet. He is turning and descending for a final pass when suddenly the ship begins receiving intense automatic weapons fire.

"Delta Six, this is Maverick Lead. LZ is too hot. Recommend you not go in."

"This is Delta Six. Negative. I'm on final . . ."

The Mavericks close around Dempsey's descending helicopter, emptying rockets into that mysterious tree line.

Delta Six peels off and lands. Almost immediately, smoke begins to billow from its tail section.

"This is Delta Six. We're hit. We're down in the LZ."

Then silence.

"Delta Six, this is Maverick Lead. Delta Six, this is Maverick Lead."

No reply.

"Delta Six is down in the LZ."

The message crackles out to Vinh Long and from there to Can Tho and Soctrang:

"Three aircraft down. Delta Six is down. Scramble all gunships . . ."

⚡

From the air: A golden brown rice paddy shimmering in the sunlight, extending as far as the eye can see. The paddy is bisected by a twisting, muddy canal bordered by lush green jungle. The jungle appears speckled with brown patches. Move in closer: They are thatched huts. Water buffalo stand at rest in the paddy — scattered around them, brown-skinned men in shorts and conical hats. Sampans glide up and down the canal. Naked children splash in the water. Timeless and peaceful. Follow the canal: The traffic dwindles, the paddies become empty of people. White smoke appears on the horizon. Then, down and to the left, three incongruous shapes. Olive green monsters from another planet — scattered around them, squirming things colored olive green. What in the . . .

Under heavy fire, Major Eberwine lands Dustoff about forty feet from Outlaw 17. The helicopters are separated by a two-foot-high dike running perpendicular to the tree line. (The whole paddy is crosshatched by dikes.) Two crewmen lie against the dike on the other side; two others lie at the base of Outlaw 17. The Dustoff crew chief, Mike Kelley, twenty-one, goes for the downed ship; Medic William Hook, twenty-four, for the two men nearest.

The slimy knee-deep mud makes for slow going. Beyond the plodding rescuers, across the paddy and over the green jungle, the sun shines incredibly bright in a powder blue sky. Bullets snap in the mud.

They get three men alongside Dustoff; Kelley is dragging the fourth when he is hit in both legs. He falls forward. Hook pulls him to the dike. Kelley says he can crawl to the aircraft. Hook races back and loads the three wounded. He fires off ten wild rounds from his carbine before it is shot from his hands. He grabs Eberwine's Thompson and shoves the bolt again and again, but it won't move. Screaming, he hurls the Thompson into the mud. The ship begins to edge forward. Kelley is crawling on board. Hook grabs his arms. Now the Viet Cong machine gun rakes across the ship. Kelley goes limp. Eberwine's left leg explodes off the tail rotor pedal and crashes into his right leg. He yells "you've got it" into the intercom to his co-pilot, Lieutenant Charles Jordan, as the helicopter jerks ninety degrees to the left, catches the toe of its right skid in the mud, and cartwheels twice and bursts into flames.

"Let's get them out!" Captain Mitchell struggles through the mud toward the burning helicopter twenty yards away,

Sergeant Bolin and their ARVN radio operator right behind him.

Eberwine unfastens his seat belt and tumbles head first over Jordan and out the door. Groggy, his left foot numb, he didn't realize the helicopter had landed on its right side. "Don't panic, just keep moving," says Jordan. Someone else from the back goes right over him. "Don't panic, now." Jordan starts to ease himself out. But he can't move. He tries again. He can't move. Finally, remembering, he unfastens his seat belt and falls out the door. Jumping to his feet, he runs to the dike, and dives. Then he remembers again. No weapon. He jumps up — bullets are impacting everywhere — and runs back and grabs his Thompson under the seat. As he turns, he notices two little figures in shorts moving near Outlaw 17. He empties his weapon at them, and dives into the mud, almost on top of Eberwine. "My leg!" Eberwine is grimacing in pain. Jordan tears away the blood-coated fatigues. An ugly white bone fragment juts from Eberwine's left leg near the calf. Jordan improvises a tourniquet from his gun sling. But he fears the tourniquet may be too tight, so he holds it with one hand, alternately squeezing and loosening, as the two men crawl away from the burning aircraft.

Approaching from the other side, Mitchell and Bolin find a crewman lying face down in the mud. It is Hook, groggy from bouncing his head off the cargo door as the aircraft flipped.

"It's good to see you, sir," Hook says. "I think the plane is going to blow up, sir. There's ammo inside, sir." Hook is moaning, trying to shout.

"Easy now," Mitchell says. "Everything is under control. Just stay down and relax." He motions to Bolin and they start to drag Hook away from the helicopter. "I'm hit," Mitchell says. "Better hand me the mike." His voice seems so calm. He reaches for the radio operator's outstretched hand, but he misses it and falls forward slowly to his knees and onto his side. "You're going to be all right, sir," Bolin says. Mitchell does not answer. The sergeant touches the young captain's right arm, it glides off his hip and drops limply into the mud, his mouth opens and closes. The bullets go snap snap.

Hook crawls toward the radio. "We've got to call for help," he says. Bolin looks at him. "We've got to call," Hook says. Bolin struggles and pulls himself out: "I just joined, I don't know the call sign to the rear . . ." He reaches into Mitchell's blouse and extracts the mud-soaked SOI tablet containing call signs. Hook grabs the mike.

"This is Dustoff eight one on the ground. We need gunships. We need air strikes on the tree line. We need . . ."

A ghostly voice crackles through the receiver.

"Do not scream on the radio. Cannot understand. Relax."

"We need air strikes, we need gunships . . ."

"Relax on the radio. Cannot understand transmission. Relax on the radio."

For a split second, the sun is blotted out. Hook feels the helicopter whoosh over him. He sees it drop onto the paddy fifty meters off. It is Delta Six.

"Don't land!" Hook shouts. "For God's sake don't land!"

"Relax . . . Cannot understand. Relax on the radio . . ."

Specialist Four William Rhodes, Delta Six crew chief, sees the windshield shatter and Dempsey flinch and slump forward in his harness. Rhodes sees it, but it doesn't really register because already the twenty-year-old crew chief is leaping, running, focusing on a figure lying prostrate twenty meters from the aircraft.

Jerry Ross, the door gunner opposite Colonel Dempsey, sees the bullet impact too. He moves toward the cockpit.

Major Casper is looking straight ahead, talking on the inter-com. "We're receiving beaucoup fire, sir. We'd better get out, sir." Then turning, seeing Dempsey: "Are you hit sir? Are you hit sir?" Suddenly the control panel goes to pieces and Casper is flung back against the door, his fatigues blot-ting red around the stomach, chest, and arm. The door flares open and Casper disappears. Ross works feverishly at Dempsey's harness. His hands turn red and sticky from what is coming from Dempsey's chest and he knows it is no use. But Casper, bleeding all over, drags himself back into the aircraft. "We've got to get the Colonel!" The ship begins to fill with smoke. In desperation, Ross shoves Casper back through the door.

Meanwhile, Rhodes works away, oblivious to everything but the mud-covered body heavy beyond belief that he finally hoists into the helicopter. "Get him out!" Ross shouts. "We're down!"

Dazedly Rhodes pulls the figure from the aircraft. This is Warrant Officer Jim Martinson, co-pilot of Outlaw 17. Were he not in shock, Martinson might have felt himself going mad. First, his ship is shot down. Then they load him on Dustoff, and it blows up. Then they load him on Delta Six and now it is smoking and they are pulling him off, back into the fire and the mud. He has been hit in the jaw and arm.

Rhodes settles Martinson alongside Casper. He pulls off belts, buckles on tourniquets. The three men start to crawl away.

"Where's Colonel Dempsey?" Casper looks about wildly.

"I don't know sir," Rhodes says.

Casper, who has taken bullets in the arm, chest, and stom-ach, turns and crawls back to the ship. Rhodes follows. Dempsey sits hunched against his harness, shrouded in the smoke that fills the cockpit and billows out the doors. Coughing and gagging, the two men try to unbuckle him.

They can't. Casper reaches up and opens Dempsey's eyes. He says, "The Colonel is dead. We'd better get out of here."

¥

There are now fourteen Americans in LZ Alpha — three helicopter crews plus two advisers. A captain and a colonel among them are dead. Most of the others are wounded. Those that can crawl away from the useless helicopters, away from the relentless machine-gun fire, to where they do not know. They crawl flat on their stomachs through foot-high paddy grass; no one can see more than a few inches ahead.

"Well, Rhodes, this looks like the reckoning day."

"Don't say that, sir."

Casper gives out what starts as a laugh. His breathing has a strange sucking sound to it.

Overhead, Skyraiders from Binh Thuy pummel the tree line. In response to a personal request from the IV Corps commander, Tactical Air Control Center in Saigon has granted an "open immediate," meaning a steady flow of air support until the request is withdrawn; planes are en route from as far away as Cam Ranh Bay in II Corps — B-57 bombers, F4C Phantoms, F-100s, Skyraiders — all for that little stretch of jungle 600 yards long and 300 yards thick fronting on LZ Alpha. Between bomb runs the helicopter gunships blast away with rockets and machine guns.

The enemy shows perfect discipline. Approaching aircraft are signaled by whistles. Fire shifts skyward. The aircraft pass. More whistles. Once again the fire plays across the paddy.

But those crawling come to adjust their movements to the whistles, too, and in this manner, one by one, they make it to a dike running parallel to the tree line about 300 yards out.

And there they huddle, pinned down, unable to comprehend how so much firepower cannot silence those machine guns. The problem also intrigues Lieutenant Rex Latham.

Latham has landed with the second lift behind a tree line 800 yards northwest of LZ Alpha; the transport ships dare not go any closer. Latham can't even see the downed helicopters. His radio is on the blink; he can't contact anyone in the air or on the ground. But he knows they are in trouble up front, that Mitchell, his commander, has been hit, and so he takes off — all five foot four inches and 130 pounds of him.

A few minutes later the circling gunships spot a lone figure breaking out of the jungle. So do the enemy machine gunners. He slogs across the open paddy, and he crawls, and somehow the little lieutenant makes it to the dike line sheltering the three crews; with them are many of the ARVN dropped with the first lift. Latham immediately takes charge of the operation on the ground. He has the wounded assembled — to be ready for possible evacuation — and directs air strikes through Bolin's radio, making like a jack-in-the-box from behind the dike.

"A little to the left . . . fifty meters maybe . . . that's it . . . that's fine."

He is moving the air strikes *away* from the tree line. The emplacements, he reports, are buried in little dike lines bracketing LZ Alpha. They are superbly hidden. One shows to be not more than fifty yards from the downed helicopters.

To Latham, it doesn't look good. Given their depth and concealment, and the shock-absorbing qualities of paddy mud, it will take some doing to silence those positions — either a succession of direct hits from the air or an assault across open ground.

Fortunately, the planners in the orbiting C&C have developed a third alternative — the 2/2 Armored Cavalry troop at that moment grinding north toward Tam Binh. Instead of heading into Hoa Binh Village as part of the original squeeze play, the Cav will ford the Mang Thit and strike across open country to LZ Alpha. What a sight: The fifteen armored vehicles assaulting across the paddy, .50s and .30s blazing, recoilless shells exploding, emplacements disintegrating, ARVN troops rising up out of the mud, charging . . . Beautiful!

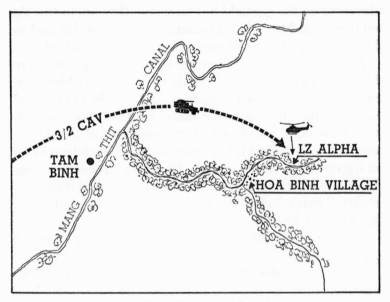

A new plan: The Cav to the rescue

The immediate problem is to keep the Viet Cong from closing on the men lying helpless behind the dike. That means almost continuous fire from the air. They can't do it without speeding up the turnaround time for gunships. Meehan radios orders for all Vinh Long ground personnel to report to the flight line.

Young Doc Hillegas can't get over it. He was transferred to Vinh Long in February, after seven months with the 1st Cavalry Division in the central highlands. There they lived behind a magnificent barrier manned by two battalions. Troops went out into the jungle fastness and were gone for days at a time.

Here the place is crawling with — Vietnamese! Over four hundred potential Viet Cong work on the base. They keep creeping up behind Doc Hillegas; it takes some getting used to. And the operations: With rare exception, they go out in the morning and return in the evening, in time to visit a few of the bars in town. And it is a lovely town, built along the calm broad Mekong River. In the evening, you can sit at the Long Chau restaurant, order giaos and beer, and contemplate the haunting lavender sunset as it plays over the sampans moving slowly across your view and on down the river into eternity, while the Beatles let loose from Long Chau's pride and joy, a Sony tape recorder.

This is the way it is in the heart of the Delta, the twenty-nine-year-old internist has come to understand. You can't go out into the jungle fastness because there isn't any. You cannot cordon yourself off from the people because they are everywhere. Shoot a bullet in the air and you are liable to hit someone you don't want to hit. Mass large numbers of troops and you are liable to get a lot of unwanted breakage. Send troops out for days, foraging off the crowded countryside, and you just might alienate the people you are meant to protect. Thus the fascinating frustration of Delta warfare: Rarely can you isolate the enemy and bring all that devastating firepower to bear.

Jon Hillegas accepts all this with a certain vague uneasiness, partly because he is such a competent doctor. He likes things clean and careful. Now this Delta war that isn't a John Wayne war, that brings him more VD cases than battle wounds . . . Well, it's for a good cause, but it sure is strange all right.

The phone rings in Hillegas's hooch, he answers . . .

Pulse decent, respiration shallow, pupils dilated . . . He does a quick cricothyroidotomy, starts intravenous fluids, and — "Get him to the flight line, fast!"

"He" is Gary Wilcox, twenty-one, a door gunner on a Soctrang slick that had gone in with the first lift. Many of the ships were riddled, but not that one. It took only one round. The bullet entered Wilcox above the right eye and exited behind the left ear.

(*"I looked around," said Kenneth Tilstra, twenty-one, the crew chief, "and there was blood spraying all over the compartment . . . the walls, the ceiling . . . everywhere. It was the wind. I rushed over and took off his helmet and put on some compresses. I held his head in my arms, you know, real tight . . . but you see it was . . . the wind. The wind was just terrible that day. The bullet kept going and cut a cable, and all the way back to Vinh Long the red master panel lights were flashing on and off. Like they were going crazy."*)

The ambulance carrying Wilcox bounces off to the flight line. A medevac helicopter, already alerted and cranking, will take him to Long Binh hospital near Saigon, fifty-five minutes away. That is standard Delta procedure. Base doctors are under orders not to fool around: Treat shock, stop hemorrhage, promote respiration, and get the patient out of there. Get him to the hospital where they have all the tools.

Jon Hillegas returns to his quarters to change from his ruined Sunday Bermudas to fatigues. Then he straps on pistol belt and canteen and heads for Outlaw operations.

The base has erupted with running men, some in Bermuda shorts, others in fatigues and T-shirts. Sergeants are moving from hooch to hooch: "All right, everybody to the flight line, on the double."

Trucks roll down the line, dropping off crates of ammo at each helicopter pad where ten-man teams crack open the crates, link ammo, cap rockets. Flight team procedures have been scrapped; the gunships return singly as soon as they have expended on target. Captain Dale Sherrod, resplendent in white shorts, white T-shirt, and tennis shoes, stands in the center of a runway fairly steaming in the 100-degree heat. Sherrod waves the incoming gunships this way and that. Fuel trucks and sandwich wagons move up, men swarm around, and off they go again. Before long, turnaround time has been cut from twenty minutes to five.

The operations shack is jammed. But quiet. They are all listening to the radio, trying to piece it together. Hillegas's request to drop into the area with first aid equipment is denied. Too dangerous, he is told. First the 2/2 Cav. Then an evacuation, probably toward noon.

Hillegas returns to the dispensary. He puts his staff to work clearing out the waiting and X-ray rooms, setting up litters, and breaking out first aid equipment. He checks over every detail. Then he goes to church.

Protestant services begin at 11:15 A.M. Hillegas feels pleased to find an overflow crowd at the base chapel. He isn't much the churchgoer himself. But he likes Easter services; he likes the hymns. Last Easter, when he was stationed at Fort Ord, in California, they drove down to Carmel, with their two little boys, to a church set back from the road in a grove of pine trees. The sharp coastal air felt wonderful. Returning, they stopped for lunch at an immaculate coffee shop. What a fine day that was. What a lovely church . . .

He wonders whether his wife has received the Easter cor-
sage. He sent it through a Honolulu mail order house. What
was it? Rusty's florist. That's right. He will have to check
on that. The service ends and Hillegas walks back to the
dispensary.

ᵂ

The Cav isn't going to make it. Major Meehan gets the
word over the radio. Forget about all that beautiful firepower. The Cav does not say as much. What they say is that
they have found the Mang Thit at low tide. The oozy mud
bank lies bare for several feet. They can't move through the
mud. They have to wait for high tide — whenever that is.

Well, Major Meehan isn't waiting for high tide. He has
three crews down there.

"Maverick Lead, this is Outlaw Six. Prepare for medevac . . ."

Major Gordon has been anticipating such a call. And trying to think of the best response. Two tours in Vietnam, un-
counted missions, but he has never met ground fire of such
intensity. The only way to avoid losing another Dustoff,
Gordon reasons, is to bring on maximum firepower at minimum range — go right in over the enemy positions with
every gunship available.

Gordon proposes to Meehan that all gunships in the area
link up in a long tactical trail formation, like a daisy chain.
Dustoff and a smoke-screen ship will come in under the trail
which will develop into an orbit pouring continuous fire on
the enemy. Meehan grants his approval.

The closer the smoke ship gets to the ground during its
runs the better. In practice, the exact level attained varies
according to the intensity of enemy fire and the temperament

of the pilot. Piloting the smoke ship (Call sign: "Viking Surprise") this Easter Sunday is Chief Warrant Officer Jerry Daley who in the past has shown himself singularly unmoved by enemy presence, thereby earning three Distinguished Flying Crosses, two Bronze Stars, a Silver Star, and the Purple Heart with oakleaf cluster. He is in fact the Delta's most decorated helicopter pilot.

Major Gordon selects a reporting point northwest of LZ Alpha for gunships, and another further north for "Viking Surprise," Dustoff, and three other impromptu medevac ships. Meehan calls for volunteers. No problem there. From the chorus, Meehan selects Major Millward, the maintenance man orbiting at 2000 feet; Major Juri Toomepuu, an Outlaw platoon leader who has just helped drop some troops nearby; and Lieutenant David Eastman who is ferrying a regimental command unit into the area.

As the Viet Cong watch from their bunkers, the gunships stop firing and swarm off to the left. In the center distance a helicopter lets go a puff of white smoke which seems to attract four other helicopters from various directions. They all buzz around for a while. Abruptly, one helicopter breaks from the swarm of gunships, another right behind it, and another, until a string of eleven gunships is moving left to right across the sky, then peeling, bearing in from the right, firing, one helicopter swooping in under the chain, coming right at them like a kamikaze. Then everything is lost in a whoosh of smoke mixed with exploding rockets and machine gun fire.

The white cloud also envelops the men behind the dike. Through this smoky haze, after a few seconds, there become discernible the shapes of four helicopters, like so many gray ghosts, hovering tentatively, gliding a little to the left, a little to the right. The men make for the helicopters, some running, others crawling, still others being carried, and as they move across the open paddy the smoke drifts away, baring the whole frantic tableau to the blazing sun and the enemy machine guns.

A southeasterly breeze is carrying the smoke away from the tree line. Daley goes into a racetrack turn for another east-west pass. He comes in right on deck and this time the defenders really open up. The helicopter shudders from multiple hits, as Daley banks clear, picks up altitude, and points for another run. With him round and round go the gunships. At the same time, Skyraiders and B-57s work the tiny tree line from west to east. The concussions from their bombs and napalm send the orbiting helicopters bouncing in the air like toys.

"Run! Run!" Hook yells for the impossible as he and Jordan struggle toward Dustoff. The medic scrambles aboard, only to turn and see Jordan lying on his face in the mud. Out he goes again. Jordan isn't hit. His feet have just sunk into the quagmire, and he has pitched forward and knocked his wind out. Hook pulls him free. Twenty yards away, Casper draws on some hidden reserve and drags himself to his feet. He staggers across the paddy to Eastman's ship. Latham pulls, shoves, and carries Americans and ARVN to Dustoff . . . First one ship reaches capacity, tilts forward, races along the ground, up, and out of LZ Alpha. Then another. Now Dustoff . . . With twelve passengers (too many), Dustoff travels about thirty yards, pauses, sinks back into the mud. It rocks clear, edges forward, and drops again. It rocks clear, gets up to fifteen feet, moving forward, speed thirty knots, then it dips, one skid catches the top of a dike, the helicopter tilts crazily, seems to stall, rocks once, twice, forward a bit, more, picking up speed, and by God they made it; the people orbiting above feel like cheering.

That leaves Toomepuu. Meehan calls for him to come out. But Toomepuu isn't listening. He isn't even in the aircraft. He is exercising in the mud. Toomepuu, his crew chief, and

gunner are struggling with the half-buried body of Eberwine. The mud seems like quicksand. Now alone in the LZ,
they are taking all the enemy's fire. But they stubbornly blot
out their imaginations and concentrate on one theme, given
voice by Toomepuu, over and over: "Okay . . . altogether
. . . we can make it . . ."

And somehow (it is a day of somehows) they do. The bul-
let-spattered ship, its radio shot out, exits safely carrying
Eberwine, and also John Martinson who is testing his fourth
helicopter of the day.

The first medevac has just put down as Doc Hillegas arrives on the line. Ground crews mill around, offering soft
drinks and sandwiches to the wounded. "Get away! Get
back!" Hillegas is furious. Someone says another medevac is
landing. "Where?" No one knows. The place is a madhouse.
Hillegas starts up the line on foot. Then he sees Major
Casper, walking away from Eastman's ship. Every visible
inch of Casper's body is caked with gray paddy mud. He is
carrying a bullet in his chest and a bullet in his midsection,
and he has bullet holes through an arm and a leg. The tall,
lanky major halts, teetering, looking down at Hillegas.

"Hi doc," he says, "I'm having a little trouble breathing."

IV

The rescue operation has been successful, but the situation on the ground still is not good. The problem lies with 3rd Battalion. The second lift (Latham's) has been placed way back from LZ Alpha, off the operation map, behind a tree line. They are disoriented. That is why Palenchar and Thanh were sent in — to effect a linkup, then launch a concerted assault.

The two majors set their sights on Latham's dike line. Toward it they direct the "lost" half of the 3/16, and two other battalions heli-lifted since — the 2/16, advancing from the west with the "lost" half, and the 1/14, advancing from the east. The idea is to link the two halves of 3rd Battalion along that dike line, bring up the other two battalions on either flank, then assault.

Second Battalion is moving south along a wooded canal — a suspected VC escape route after the nighttime attack. Though LZ Alpha is a good 800 meters to their left front, 2nd Battalion is drawing fire from their right. It seems the Viet Cong have snipers in bunkers and spider holes on that canal too!

By 4:00 P.M., 2nd Battalion has cleared the finger canal and secured the right flank. Then, feeling their oats, their own right wing begins an envelopment. Meanwhile, Palenchar frantically tries to organize a center assault across the open paddy. But there are these machine guns that keep returning to life after each bomb run. Palenchar and Thanh

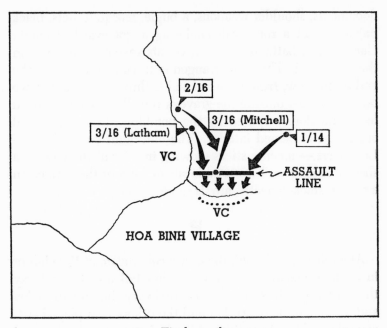

Final assault

get the men forward a few feet at a time to another dike 100 meters from the smoking tree line. There they are stopped cold. Each time they make to move, a machine gun on the left lets go. It reaches 6:00 P.M., an hour short of darkness. The exasperated Palenchar takes his radio operator way around to the left, crawling, to within forty meters of the troublesome bunker. He gets the gunships on the radio. The first rocket sails smack into the gun slit. Palenchar can hardly contain himself. All the gunship pilots hear is: "Beautiful! . . . Beautifulbeautifulbeautiful!! . . ."

And so, as night closes around the retreating Viet Cong survivors, the men of 9th Division move into the nearly bombed-out tree line. There, amongst the craters and grotesquely cleaved trees, they find 142 enemy dead, piles of documents, shoulder weapons, a bugle, mosquito nets, black pajamas, and a rock wall enclosing a graveyard. Captain Gary Luff, a battalion adviser, counts seventeen mounds in the graveyard. They are arranged in three neat rows. At the end of one row, freshly turned soil is thrown up around two open pits. Just outside the graveyard wall stands a thatched hut miraculously spared by the bombing. Luff stoops and enters the darkened interior. The only light comes from — Luff peers — incense sticks glowing in a jar at the base of a shrine. A long well-worn table sits in front of the shrine. In a corner, stacked neatly, are six sanded caskets.

≅

At Vinh Long airfield, the crews congregate at the club or in small groups in their quarters. They talk about how lucky they are, about hits taken by nearly every ship, about Daley and Toomepuu and Gordon and the others who played special roles — like Major Bill Gebhardt, Lancer Lead, who went into LZ Alpha without smoke cover, after a post-rescue head count showed that Jon Myrhe, pilot of Outlaw 17, was still missing. Mostly they talk about twenty-one-year-old Myrhe, one of the most popular men in the company. Myrhe had been scheduled to leave Tuesday for a six-day reunion with his wife in Honolulu. Someone will have to call her.

Part of the Dustoff crew gather on the flight line. They smoke and gaze idly down the runway lined with silent helicopters. The place seems oddly deserted now, like a football stadium on Saturday night. Hook, the medic, sits there alone with himself, and the machine guns, and his friend, Kelley, going limp and falling away . . . Kelley . . . Why Kelley?

Then: A familiar thumping in the distance. Must be those

gunships coming home, someone says. Colonel Charles
Davis, IV Corps deputy senior adviser, up for a briefing, had
headed back to Can Tho an hour earlier escorted by two
Vinh Long gunships. The thumping grows louder. There
they are, someone says. The blinking red navigation lights
come into view. There's three of them, someone says.
Wonder why? They approach from the east in trail forma-
tion. A slick with the IV Corps insignia leads the way.
Wonder why Colonel Davis is still with them, someone says.
The IV Corps slick drifts to rest about fifty yards from the
Dustoff crew. What's going on there, someone says. Hook is
up and running. They are unloading a body.

Hillegas drives up in the ambulance. He shines a flash-
light over the mud-coated figure lying face down on a
stretcher.

"Kelley!" Hook shouts. "Kelley! It's Kelley!"

The figure stirs.

"What is your name?" Hillegas asks.

The voice is barely audible. "Jon Myrhe," it says.

"You're Kelley! You're Kelley!"

The voice becomes stronger. "Jon Myrhe," it says, "Outlaw one seven."

(Myrhe is suffering from shock, a broken leg, and a shat-
tered pelvis. Such was the initial — and correct — diagnosis
of Captain Bruce Wiita from 3000 feet. Wiita is a medical
officer at Binh Thuy. He went up with Spooky 51 that night,
just for kicks. They were circling LZ Alpha, dropping flares,
when they intercepted a radio report from Latham to Palenchar. Latham, searching LZ Alpha for dead and wounded,
said he had come upon an American in great pain; he was
afraid to move him. Dr. Wiita got on the radio to Latham.
After providing the diagnosis, Spooky 51 doubled back to

Binh Thuy and collected some morphine for Myrhe which they dropped into LZ Alpha. A while later, the Davis party came by and the young pilot was extracted.)

They carry Myrhe into the dispensary's brightly lit treatment room. Hillegas goes to work. Word of the rescue spreads quickly. In no time the hallway and waiting room are jammed. There is a scuffle outside . . . "No, Ray, Doc says no one inside. Ray!" Captain Ray Leuty bursts into the room. Leuty is Myrhe's big burly platoon leader. His eyes are wet and blinking. "I can't believe it . . . I can't believe it . . ." Awkwardly, he grabs Myrhe's hand.

"C'mon Ray," Meehan says, "it's all right. He'll be okay."

"Doc?"

"Sure Ray," Hillegas says. "I'm sending him to the hospital in Long Binh. He'll be okay."

They drive Myrhe out to the line and load him onto the medevac ship. On impulse, Hillegas pulls himself aboard. The helicopter lifts softly off the pad and floats up and up into the darkness. The airfield perimeter lights fade to little sparks. The air turns cool and fresh, it tastes wonderful. Hillegas lights a cigarette. He exhales slowly, carefully, his chin on one hand, his gaze settling on the wet rice paddies that float way off to the horizon. The full moon makes little pools of mercury in the paddies. Hillegas watches the pools, enchanted.

V

Consider these details: On Easter Eve the Viet Cong jammed Vinh Long sector frequency, roadblocked the route to Caumoy Bridge, launched a light attack with mortars and automatic weapons on the Caumoy regimental CP, a heavy mortar and recoilless rifle attack on Tam Binh district town, and a full scale assault on 1st Battalion — all coordinated. They then retreated in order along a guarded route to prepared positions from which they destroyed three helicopters and held elements of four ARVN battalions at bay for several hours in broad daylight despite constant air bombardment. Their machine gun positions were set for enfilade and so well concealed that a good part of the bombardment was wasted on empty jungle. More: 1st Battalion, probing out on Easter morning, found communications wire all around; the attacking half-naked guerrillas had telephones.

In short, the Viet Cong attack was planned and executed by professionals — revolutionaries, yes, but of a sort who would be hard put to find a place in their ranks for a Guevara or a Zapata or a Garibaldi, or even a Tito or a Ben Bella. The main difference between this revolutionary movement and those others is in a word: Time. The Viet Cong have been active in the Delta for more than twenty years. Theirs has not been the standard metamorphosis of successful revolutionary movements: Idea to Action to Victory to Consolidation-midst-purge-and-confusion. The Viet Cong reached the second point — "Action" — and held it. They gave to "Action" an extraordinary form and permanence. They institutionalized it. The Viet Cong can be less understood as a guerilla army than as an exquisitely developed clandestine organization.

The Viet Cong organization parallels the South Vietnamese government in the Delta from Region to province to village, like this:

Region. The sixteen provinces form a Region governed by a Viet Cong civilian-military committee. The committee exercises direct control over two regiments, three battalions each — the DT-1 regiment based fifty miles south of Saigon, and the D-2 regiment based in the southernmost U Minh forest along the Gulf of Siam. The regiments do not function as integrated units; assignments are addressed to individual battalions. These six so-called "main force" battalions are the Viet Cong elite. Wherever they go — and they can go anywhere in the Region — local units provide food and lodging.

Province. The Viet Cong "provincial mobile" battalion, at the next level of command, operates only in its home province at the discretion of the provincial civilian-military committee.

District. The Viet Cong district committee directs a multi-platoon District Concentrated Unit (DCU) of from forty to one hundred men. The DCU's primary missions are road interdiction, harassment of government outposts and offices, and security: When district officials move, the DCU screens; when district officials stop for meetings or propaganda lectures, the DCU sets up a floating perimeter.

Village. The village committee musters a squad of from six to twenty men who fabricate grenade traps and pointed bamboo "punji" stakes, provide security for couriers and village political officers, and sometimes fire on small government outposts.

Except in unusual circumstances, the village squad operates only in its village and the DCU only in its district.[2]

At the lowest level are the unarmed part-time village guerrillas, who occupy themselves, when they are not farming, with hauling and storing ammunition, digging bunkers, preparing propaganda tools, etc.

The whole system is geared for quick small-unit thrusts. Toward this end, battalions are split up into independently operating companies, though they occasionally mass for an attack on a major outpost. That occasion, it should be emphasized, is extremely rare. Even the main force battalions, the elite units, seldom strike in battalion strength. For instance in Vinh Long province, in the heart of the Delta, where an estimated 6000 Viet Cong are operating, including one provincial battalion and one main force battalion, the year 1967 produced one battalion-size engagement. During the same period, 1024 "incidents" were recorded, most of them roadblocks, assassinations, minings, ambushes, and attacks on small outposts. Those were the conspicuous incidents. Hundreds, probably thousands, of more subtle enemy actions went unrecorded in Vinh Long. The Viet Cong operate mobile tax collection posts, they offer public lectures and plays, they conduct recruiting drives. On one known occasion in Vinh Long they administered cholera shots to the people in a hamlet. Another time a Viet Cong cadre indemnified peasants in cash for damage received when American helicopters strafed their village while a Viet Cong unit was resting there. One evening they blew up the house of a gov-

---

[2] In February 1967, these units were armed as follows:

    Battalion — .60- and .81-mm. mortars, .30- and .50-caliber machine guns, a variety of recoilless rifles, from the Russian B-40 to the U.S. .75, and a whole panoply of hand weapons — Chinese, Russian, Czech, French, American.

    DCU — Carbines, M-1 rifles, submachine guns, automatic rifles, and sometimes, .30-caliber machine guns and .60-mm. mortars.

    Village squad — Carbines, M-1 rifles, and an occasional submachine gun. Also employed are homemade weapons, grenades, and mines.

ernment counterintelligence agent, killing his wife and two children.

Thus, when night falls in the Delta and the curfew goes into effect, as traffic halts on the roads and sampans are beached on canals, as the bright green jungle canopy along the canals blurs to black and the glistening rice paddies to a somber gray, as a deadly stillness settles over the whole ensemble, the Viet Cong begin to move. Couriers are dispatched, political cadre meet in dark huts, tax collectors go forth into villages, assassination teams bear down on marked officials, small units set up ambushes on roads and canals, big units close on outposts and other fortifications. To suddenly push away the night in the Delta would be like turning up the underside of a damp log — all silence and innocence on one side, quivering with activity on the other.

VI

The intricately organized attack on Easter Sunday is best appreciated, then, not as an isolated incident, but as a rather violent pulsation issuing from a weblike system that blankets the Delta. One of the two Viet Cong prisoners captured on Easter Sunday, sixteen-year-old, Nguyen Van Bacv, talked most revealingly about his entry into the web and his passage through it to Vinh Long. Nguyen's point of entry was Dong Thai village, Kien Giang province, eighty miles southwest of Vinh Long. A summary of his account follows.[3]

·

[3] I obtained this account during four separate interviews with the youth over a period of six weeks. He seemed willing to talk. He was not "hard core." He had been recruited less than three months before his capture.

One evening in January, Nguyen joined 200 of his fellow
villagers for a performance by an itinerant drama team. The
first number was a skit. It opened on a group of peasants at
work in their rice paddy. Suddenly a team of men in olive
green uniforms rushed onto the stage. The peasants tried to
run but they were quickly surrounded. Enter a huge ugly
man wearing a ludicrous tin nose and brandishing a pistol.
The green-clad soldiers bowed before the giant, then turned
on the peasants and commenced beating them. The giant
looked on with evident satisfaction. He shouted "Okay!
Okay! Okay!" and fired his pistol again and again into the air.
The audience booed and hissed. And another road triumph
was recorded by the Kien Giang provincial drama team of
the Viet Cong.

The program closed with a speech by a political commissar, himself a native of Kien Giang. The so-called government officials call us invaders, the commissar said, but how
can we invade our own province? The government officials talk of "invasion," yet who takes orders from American
foreigners? Did the people invite these foreigners? Did you
invite them? Government officials invited them. The same
officials who travel in trucks, armored cars, and airplanes. Is
that how the people travel? The people travel like we
do, in sampans and on foot. The people eat like we do,
not at huge banquets. The people sleep like we do, not in
forts and castles built by French colonialists. We are the
people's vanguard. Come join us in the struggle to free our
nation from foreign domination . . .

Thirty youths were recruited. Nguyen joined for excitement, others out of conviction, still others from fear of reprisal; the proportion probably varies from village to village
in the Delta. In this area — shown on government maps as
VC-controlled — the "conviction" ratio is probably higher
than elsewhere. Once, when a nearby government outpost

came under Viet Cong attack, the village was mistakenly bombed by government aircraft.

Nguyen and his fellow recruits left Dong Thai the following night, escorted by a dozen armed Viet Cong cadre. Each recruit was issued a rucksack, a set of black pajamas, five liters of rice, a shovel, and a poncho. They walked barefoot, usually along the jungled canals. At dawn, before going to sleep, they dug foxholes alongside their ponchos.

On the second day, a single engine spotter plane swooped down low, and soon helicopter gunships arrived and the young initiates, cowering in their foxholes, received their baptism under fire. No one was hurt. Hours later, as they moved in darkness along a canal, the gunships returned, alerted this time, they were told, by an informer in one of the hamlets they had traversed. Again, they were lucky.

On the evening of the fourth day, the chief cadre delivered the youngsters a stern lecture. They were gathered in a hut on the edge of the biggest canal Nguyen had ever seen. The opposite bank was barely visible.

A junk will come for us, a cadre said. We will climb inside and lie down and not move or make a sound. Not a sound. If anyone shoots, lie still. If someone is hit, he will not shout. If something happens and you are captured, say nothing. If you talk, they will kill you.

Toward midnight the junk appeared as promised. They were ushered aboard, whereupon each youngster, full of fear and excitement, lay down and turned himself to stone, as the junk edged slowly into open water.

This was the Bassac River, southern wing of the great Mekong, flowing across the Delta into the South China Sea. The Bassac is patrolled night and day by high-speed U.S. Navy PBR boats, armed with mortars and .50-caliber machine guns. Sometimes they catch Viet Cong crossing the river.

This time they didn't. On the opposite bank, the travelers

were met by more cadre. They were guided to a village and, as dawn broke, to bed.

That evening, before resuming the march, the chief cadre announced they were in Vinh Long province and that in two or three days they would join their assigned unit, the 306th regional main force battalion. There were murmurs of excitement. The famous 306th! In Dong Thai, its exploits were legendary.

Eight days after leaving Dong Thai, the group arrived in Cang Long district, Vinh Binh province (adjoining Vinh Long), base camp of the 509th provincial mobile battalion, temporary resting place for units of the 306th.[4]

Nguyen was assigned to 57 Company (306 Bn.) as a cook and BAR ammo carrier. The following night the company moved out and Nguyen's training began. He learned how to run on his toes over rice paddies — so as not to make splashing noises in the mud — to crawl, dig bunkers, strip and clean shoulder weapons. The schedule was harsh. Generally, it meant getting up every morning at 5:00 A.M. for calisthenics, then breakfast. Training from seven to ten. Sleep till one. Lunch. Back to sleep. Move out to next objective at 5:00 P.M. Missions until 2:00 or 3:00 A.M., then sleep. Sometimes those on missions stayed out all night.

Nguyen always remained at camp, cooking rice and digging foxholes. The battalion provided the rice, the men fished the canals and paddies for the rest of their diet. (The porous delta mud nurtures small fish; quite tasty.)

---

[4] A document captured on Easter Sunday suggests that the web over which Nguyen traveled even reaches inside the government: The document states that the 306th Battalion was sent to Vinh Long in December to disrupt the upcoming Mang Thit pacification campaign.

The captured document reads in part: "The enemy plans to reopen the front line at the Mang Thit and reoccupy it. But the Mang Thit is a main center of our activity. For this reason, we must concentrate our effort to defeat the enemy."

The Mang Thit campaign was then in the top-secret planning stage.

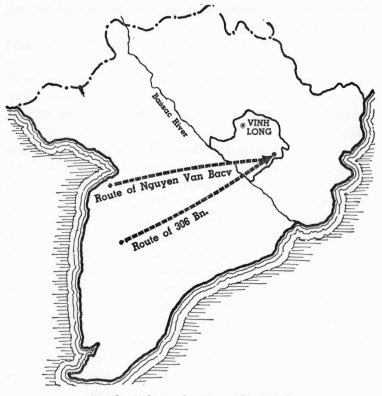

Up the Delta to the Mang Thit Canal

Never did 57 Company spend more than twenty-four hours at any given location. Indeed, never did Nguyen see 306 Battalion assembled as a unit. His "world" consisted of the eighty-five men of 57 Company.

On March 25, the day before Easter, 57 Company was quartered in Hoa Binh Village, Tra On District, Vinh Long province. Late that afternoon everyone gathered before a hand-sketched map for a briefing by the company commander. Nguyen knew this mission was important because for the first time the map showed 57 Company as just one attacking unit among several.

After the briefing the men dined on fish and rice, then went to work on their weapons. The platoon leaders inspected each piece. Those men designated to participate in the attack exchanged black pajamas for shorts. At dusk, about a dozen sampans appeared. The half-naked men climbed aboard. Equipment clattered, came to rest. The sampans moved silently up the canal and disappeared into the gathering darkness.

The attack on 1st Battalion was about to begin.

It is failure — perhaps refusal — to grasp the full dimensions of this extraordinary web that accounts for the mistaken hopes and pronouncements that followed the government victory on Easter Sunday. When the web is cut in places — as happened on Easter Sunday — signals go out and an invisible mending process begins. The process may take months, during which time quiet reigns over that particular part of the countryside, glowing reports flow into Saigon, where they are tabulated and forwarded to Washington. Progress in Vinh Long! But all the while the breach is being quietly repaired. And one morning the local government wakes up to find that "X" district which was declared pacified is making trouble again, or "X" Viet Cong unit which was pronounced "eliminated as a fighting force" has just launched a major attack.

PART THREE

The (So-Called) Tet Offensive

I

U.S.-ARVN: The Psycho-Strategic Response

IF MILITARY BRIEFERS were judged like movie stars, Brigadier General William Desobry might have won an Oscar for his performance in Saigon on January 9, 1968. His work with the pointer was superb; for special emphasis he would move to the wall map and with a grease pencil circle a strategic site: Viet Cong D857 Battalion — here! Vinh Binh commo-liaison route — here! The facts and figures poured forth with soothing assurance — the names of enemy units, their exact location, their strength, their armament, their objectives, even the level of their morale ("poorly motivated, poorly trained"). Desobry was talking about Viet Cong in IV Corps, the Mekong Delta, where he had commanded the U.S. advisory effort for the past two and a half years. This was his farewell press briefing before reassignment to America. He concluded:

"So in sum I find that in the Delta there has been considerable progress. I think that now ARVN has the upper hand completely, and I think that the Viet Cong are going down steadily. I think the pacification program, the RD program, has taken hold, there have been some significant successes, and I think that this significant success in the military situation will permit ARVN to move ahead in 1968 to much faster progress than we've already had previously."

Less than three weeks later, Desobry's "poorly motivated, poorly trained" Viet Cong simultaneously struck thirteen of the Delta's sixteen province capitals, then withdrew, leaving behind mountains of rubble, 1100 dead civilians, 5600 wounded civilians, 107,000 refugees. In the provinces where the Viet Cong concentrated their attacks, Desobry's offensive-minded ARVN ("the upper hand completely") abandoned the countryside and regrouped around the cities.

How could Our Man in the Delta have been so wrong? Was he covering up? Or was he simply unaware of what was happening? Probably a combination of both. Covering up exists by another name in Vietnam. It is called "optimism." The psychology of Vietnam optimism, with its special emphasis on repression and the self-fulfilling prophecy, will be discussed later. What is relevant here is the degree to which the demonstrated ignorance of the Delta's senior American was tied to a failure to understand the enemy.

General Desobry's briefing included an evaluation of the battle on Easter Sunday in which he makes this point: "Since Easter the [Viet Cong] 306th [Battalion] has broken up into small units . . . We have obviously gained the upper hand over the 306th Main Force Battalion."

General Desobry's evaluation ignores the enemy's basic commitment to small unit tactics. The 306th was *always* "broken up" into small units. Throughout 1967, the 306th only fought as a battalion once — on Easter Sunday. A few hours later, it reestablished its normal order of battle: four independently operating companies.

The distortions encouraged by this basic misunderstanding of Viet Cong tactics in the Delta are compounded by distortions resulting from our psychological commitment to a mystical something known as "rapport." The self-denying influences of "rapport" showed up in the official evaluation of the Easter Sunday battle.

After the landing under fire of the first troop lift, that engagement developed as a classic assault against an entrenched enemy unit. At last, the enemy had come out from his dark hole and we had him, trapped, in broad daylight. We immediately brought to bear air power, artillery, and a vastly superior ground force.

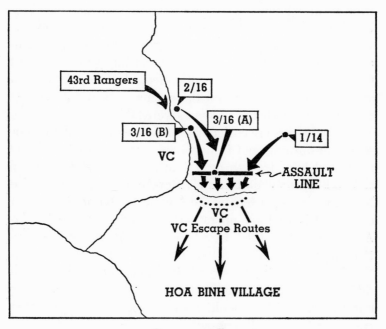

One-way traffic

The map shows the disposition of forces. First came a company from 3rd Battalion, 16th Regiment. Next, the remainder of 3rd Battalion, 600 yards to the northwest. Next, 1st Battalion, 14th Regiment, 800 yards back and to the east.

Next, 2nd Battalion, 16th Regiment, *behind* 3rd Battalion. Finally, the 43rd Rangers, way off to the northwest.

Down from the north came four ARVN battalions. When night fell the Viet Cong withdrew to the south. ARVN did not pursue. Next morning, ARVN searched the enemy's abandoned positions. At noon they were heli-lifted back to their distant bases.

The kill-ratio measurement institutionalized by the MACV command guarantees a kind of victory in any head-on encounter in Vietnam, and Easter Sunday was no exception. Tactically, however, the battle was a failure. The enemy was trapped in broad daylight. Escape routes were obvious and limited. There was plenty of time; the entrenched Viet Cong should have been surrounded. Instead, ARVN assaulted from the north and the enemy walked out through the back door; only two prisoners were taken.

Tactical errors are correctable: A weak commander can be replaced; misjudgment in deployment can be reviewed and converted into strength next time around. Helpful toward this end is the standard-form "After-Action" report compiled for higher headquarters by the American advisory team after each ARVN division operation. Interestingly, the "After-Action" report for the Easter Sunday battle contains no mention of General Thi's gross tactical error, not even in the section labeled "Lessons Learned" included to expose just such difficulties. In this instance, the distortion occurred because our advisers' critical faculties were neutralized by a higher consideration, namely "rapport."

"Rapport" — a word for the relationship between the U.S. adviser and his ARVN counterpart — can only be understood in its operative context, i.e., the strange world of General Thi and his fellow ARVN commanders. General Thi's superiors have assigned him a role that is only partly military. In his 9th Division Tactical Area (DTA), encompassing six provinces, General Thi reigns like a viceroy. Major decisions are channeled through his office. The six province chiefs in his DTA are colonels, his subordinates in military rank and governmental status.[1] This means that General Thi is rated on his political performance within the military establishment that rules the civil government.

General Thi's unusual political-military position is a product of a generation of war which has opened to the military a path into politics and *from there* into power. Once in power, at the head of a Division for instance, the challenge is not so much to overwhelm the enemy — a military challenge — as it is to remain in power — a political challenge.

During my stay in Vinh Long, General Thi showed a consistent reluctance to close with the Viet Cong. Who could blame him? The Viet Cong do not constitute a direct threat to his power. The chief threat to his power is political. It comes from within a factionalized military government in which the nomination of key officeholders — Province Chiefs, Division commanders, Corps commanders — emerges out of the complex maneuverings of competing politico-generals. In the Delta, the military hero figure is not the successful warrior but the *political* general who retains his *political* command while others are falling on the *political* battlefield.

The unspoken motto of ARVN 9th Division, then, is not victory. It is persistence.

Enter the American adviser. Advice is a form of criticism. An adviser by definition is a critic. In Vietnam, however, the American adviser-as-critic finds himself in conflict with his primary mission: To establish a confidential relationship

[1] On government charts, Province Chiefs are shown as reporting directly to Saigon. In the 9th DTA, this was a fiction. It is self-delusion to suppose that a military government would grant colonels priority over generals. The ARVN web operates independently of the administrative decrees that American advisers often take such pleasure in citing.

with his counterpart. Without this "rapport," nothing can go forward. The adviser who alienates his counterpart only neutralizes his own effectiveness as an adviser.

To meet the above-defined mission, the adviser modifies his professional instincts, rationalization sets in, and a subtle change occurs. The adviser may not be conscious of it. He sees himself as encouraging his counterpart to bolder action by emphasizing the positive. But what has happened is that the adviser-as-critic has given way to the adviser-as-morale-builder.

The adviser-as-morale-builder overlooks errors in the interest of "rapport." The ARVN general knows this and plays on it. The American encourages and the ARVN general smiles, "rapport" is strengthened and everyone is happy. Mark up a victory for persistence.

The helicopter — a popular symbol of counterinsurgency mobility — is employed in the Delta in a way that dramatizes the clash between American strategy of victory and ARVN strategy of persistence. Helicopter mobility is most effective, and beautiful to watch, when used with aggressive ground units. A small unit makes contact and a reaction force is quickly lifted in. The enemy never knows how many troops he will be taking on. Rarely did General Thi use his helicopters in this manner. (On Easter Sunday, helicopter support followed an attack on a defensive position and persistence modified victory in other ways.) Under General Thi, helicopter pilots earned their pay ferrying troops on flamboyant operations involving many ARVN and few Viet Cong.

The heli-lifted operation begins at the Landing Zone (LZ) and ends at the Pickup Zone (PZ). On the operation map the preplanned route is marked with a series of "objectives." Unit commanders radio their location by saying, "We are 200 meters south of Objective Four," etc. The operation plan calls for final helicopter pickup at a certain time, usually in the late afternoon. I witnessed many of these operations. They have a way of turning into a race to the Pickup Zone. The idea is to arrive "on schedule" to be picked up by the helicopters. The procedure does not encourage careful searching for the enemy. If a unit is running behind schedule, its commander has no qualms about skirting suspicious areas on his line of march so as not to be late for the afternoon helicopter home.

Helicopters originally were made available to improve ARVN mobility. But they won't work because the problem is not mobility, the problem is the strategy of Persistence. Helicopters simply provide ARVN with more comfortable vehicles to travel down the same road.

It seems clear that criticism finds little nourishment in a society peopled with morale-building U.S. advisers and defensive (in thought and deed) ARVN officers. What about Viet Cong society?

One would expect the criticism spirit to experience rough going in this clandestine outlaw organization ruled by strict ideologists imbued with concepts like "thought control" and "collectivism" (as opposed to our "free expression" and "individualism"). Yet the spirit survives among the Viet Cong. It flourishes. It permeates the organization in measures almost obsessive. Here are a few thoughts lifted verbatim from a notebook captured Easter Sunday, belonging to an officer-cadre of 306th Battalion. The observations were jotted down over a four-month period.

Deficiencies: Failure to thoroughly understand the ideology of destroying the enemy and strengthening our force. This was evidenced by the fact that our troops did not collect enough weapons when they destroyed 1D . . .

Units should try to overcome difficulties without bothering higher echelon. This will enable the latter to better serve them . . .

Members should have a better attitude and morale. Avoid dodging work and hesitation to sacrifice . . .

Training on two tactics of raids and ambushes. The use of three infantry c's to attack the post is excessive.

Particular attention should be paid to the attitude of soldiers toward the people . . .

In order to insure combat tactics troops must be neatly and lightly equipped. For they have to move with great *mobility* . . .[2]

Essential factors leading us to victory are: cover and surprising attacks in which troops must always keep the initiative to assault the enemy when the opportunity arises . . .

[The battalion's] missions must stay close to local political missions. . . .

Considering the rear service mission and the general policies of higher echelons, all units are requested:
    –to popularize the ideology of economy and honesty.
    –to be tolerant of corruption and waste.
    –to maintain carefully both equipment and clothing . . .

The self-complacency of cadre is still present . . . Self-complacency regarding past achievements has been discovered within units.

Use ammunition economically . . .

---

[2] Note the Viet Cong definition of mobility ("lightly equipped") as opposed to ours (trucks, helicopters, etc.).

Counter against mechanistic and simplistic doctrines. People must be stimulated to study.

Counter against the spirit of setting a high value on combat and a low level on building . . .

Prevent soldiers from becoming jealous and envious of one another . . .

Instill a high spirit of responsibility in doing any task. Do not do something as a matter of form . . .

Guard against proud soldiers who are sufficient to themselves and who don't like to learn . . .

Counter waste and corruption. Stress economy . . .

Signs of overconfidence appear, attitudes are deplorable, lack of respect for punctuality and time while in activities . . .

Attitude during the activities, names, greeting and treatment, lack of modesty among fellows. Clothing was worn sloppily; the attitude of forty members and cadre is haughty and bullying toward the people. They swore when they met with difficulties in performance, thus dissatisfying the people . . .

Investigation was not thoroughly made. As a result, deployment of troops was poorly made during assaults. It is therefore requested that the unit be additionally trained . . .

1. Improve the attitudes of unit members to behave properly during Tet.
2. Keep them from criticizing or laughing at the people.
3. Strengthen the unit with the people. Cadre should teach members to behave properly.

Despite "thought control" at every level, criticism flourishes within the Viet Cong organization. Despite homage to "free expression," criticism suffers among U.S.-ARVN. The apparent contradiction can be resolved, I think, by studying the different rules imposed by the "game" each side is playing.

The Viet Cong officer writes: "The use of three infantry c's [companies] to attack the post is excessive . . . Counter waste and corruption. Stress economy . . ."

The Viet Cong operate in a condition of scarcity. They must practice economy if they are to survive. The effect has been to make economy both a strategic necessity and a moral virtue. This is healthy climate for criticism.

ARVN, on the other hand, operates at the mouth of a cornucopia. Wedded to the belief that technology brings progress, Americans make its fruits available in abundance. (Among "optimists" more matériel is described as a "positive" response to the problem, as opposed to criticism, a "negative" response.) The result is a papering-over of the crucial difference between our desire to win the war and the desire of ARVN commanders to persist in power. Technology does the job by creating an illusory aura. In order to encourage ARVN commanders, we permit them to draw lavishly on our technological resources. Deployment of these resources, as with helicopters, fosters an illusion of aggressiveness. The illusion soothes our troubled spirit. If they are moving they *must* be aggressive. The chop chop of the colorful whirlybirds and the endless spin and tumble of troops work on the advisers like psychedelic tranquilizers. Now *we* feel encouraged.

Two different worlds. No, three. Viet Cong, ARVN, U.S. advisers. To the Americans the object of the game is victory. Our error begins with the assumption that ARVN shares our objective. Everything that follows, no matter how well-intentioned, takes us further from our goal.

Our policy can be compared to that of a group of investment counselors who kept channeling money into a corrupt enterprise. In the beginning, when the company's structural weaknesses were recognized, the counselors decided that the problem could be cured with funds and equipment. These were provided. At first, reports were encouraging. Then the company began to slide. At this point, the counselors found that to the initial requirement — strengthening the company — had been added two more requirements: (1) to protect their investment; (2) to protect their reputations as investment counselors. Gradually, as the financial stakes increased and as criticism of investment policy developed, the second two requirements began to weigh more heavily than the first. This was not always a conscious process. It surfaced, under pressure, as a rationale: "The company is on the verge of astounding success, there is light at the end of the tunnel, all the company needs right now is a bit more funds and equipment to maintain momentum, and, above all, the company needs encouragement." Again, funds and equipment were forthcoming. But with the broadening of the investment base came an increase in outside criticism about investment policy. The response was a magnification of the rationale. Now, more than ever, the investors were defending the spirit of optimism that had determined the nature of the commitment. That is, they were no longer defending the company, they were defending themselves. And so, the word went out to the counselors' representatives in the field: "We are providing more funds and equipment. But it will all be to naught without a third *essential* ingredient which is encouragement." Thus, success was made *contingent upon* encouragement. The old spirit of optimism had evolved into official policy. It had been institutionalized as an end in itself. Criticism was stifled.

.

Three months after the Easter battle, Defense Secretary McNamara, on one of his periodic fact-finding missions, visited the 9th DTA for a briefing by General Thi.

"I am going to confine my briefing," General Thi began, "to one particular aspect of the revolutionary development program in the Division Tactical Area. That is the opening of the Mang Thit River–Nicolai Canal." [3]

Thi explained the strategic importance of the canal. He outlined government efforts to wrest it from Viet Cong control. "An important turning point," Thi said, "came on Easter Sunday . . ."

With those words, the Easter Sunday battle entered the folklore. Now it was to be celebrated with appropriate reverence and fervor at briefings in Vinh Long, at 9th Division headquarters in Sadec, at IV Corps headquarters in Can Tho, at MACV headquarters in Saigon.

The "turning point" on Easter Sunday was in our minds. It was dictated by Division Logic. But the situation on the ground was quite different from the situation in our minds. The difference increased until finally, in February 1968, the whole distorted picture exploded in our faces. Before recounting this progressive flight from reality, further explanation of our military posture in Vinh Long is necessary.

The Easter Sunday battle (as I have said), was not typical of warfare in the Delta. There the war was fought in hundreds of tiny engagements that never made the briefings and were recorded at the province Tactical Operations Center (TOC) as "incidents."

The most common incidents were attacks on government outposts. Vinh Long had 290 outposts, ranging from lonely watchtowers that thrust up like outsized anthills along roads and bridges, to spacious triangular mud-walled enclosures around village offices. Each watchtower was guarded by six

[3] For the full text of this briefing, see Appendix D p. 215.

to twelve men, each fortified office by twenty to forty men. The defenders were provincial militia, either Popular Forces (PF), who were recruited and assigned in their home district, or Regional Forces (RF), who could be assigned anywhere in their home province.

The impact of these outposts on the conduct of the war can be summed up in a number: 7000. In Vinh Long, 7000 RF/PF were assigned to outposts from a total province RF/PF strength of 10,000. This meant that 70 percent of the troops under the Province Chief's command were engaged in static defense. An additional 1000 troops had administrative assignments, leaving only 2000, or 20 percent that could be called mobile forces.

What's worse, an outpost is not a self-sustaining enterprise. Its occupants must be kept regularly supplied with food and ammunition. The mobile forces in Vinh Long spent a good deal of their time resupplying outposts. It got to be like a game. For instance, one road in Vinh Long was "secured" by a string of seven outposts. The Viet Cong, ignoring the outposts, sealed off both ends of the road in 1965. Thereafter, the only traffic consisted of an occasional heavily armed resupply convoy for the seven isolated outposts "protecting" the untraveled road.[4]

Some American advisers suggested that the outposts — relics of the French colonial period — be "consolidated" (reduced in number), thereby freeing more soldiers for offensive combat. But the Vietnamese officers who ruled on such matters had become attached to the outposts as they

[4] The pacification campaign along the Mang Thit–Nicolai Canal in Vinh Long included the construction of 11 new outposts, bringing the number of outposts along that 28-mile waterway to 32, each staffed with a PF platoon. An American adviser living in a district bordering the Mang Thit suggested to me that the planners weren't thinking big enough. "Eleven new outposts won't do it," he said. "What we need is a wall. Something like the Great Wall of China, with watchtowers every fifty feet."

had become attached to French cognac and (more recently)
PX whisky.

When the Vietnamese balked at outpost reform, the mor-
rale-building mystique took over. The outposts became a
"symbol" of government strength; their destruction, it was
argued, would affect "morale." So we strengthened the outposts. In Vinh Long, many isolated outposts were resupplied
by U.S. helicopters — another case of mobility in action
against itself.[5]

In Vinh Long province those 290 outposts stood out as the
most original contribution to Delta warfare of the strategy of
Persistence. No one could be criticized from on high for losing an insignificant little outpost; there were hundreds of
them. Meanwhile, Viet Cong attacks on outposts helped cre-
ate an illusion of activity on the briefing charts. (Viet Cong
tried to take six outposts last night, the briefer would say,
but were defeated every time.)

So far I have discussed two extremes on the Persistence
strategy scale — Outposts and Division operations. A vast
middle ground was exploited by Sector (i.e., Province) and
District operations, which ran like those of Division, but on a
progressively smaller scale. As with Division, a Sector or
District foray sometimes turned up Viet Cong, but more
often it developed into a long walk through grasping paddy
mud under a wilting sun. A battalion (at most, two) and
perhaps a troop of armored cavalry might be involved in a
Sector operation. At the District level, where mobile forces
were few, outpost personnel participated in the operations.[6]

---

[5] Shortly after the February 1968 Tet offensive, while visiting a Vinh Long
subsector team, I learned of a helicopter pilot who, upon descending
through light sniper fire to land supplies for an outpost a few days earlier,
found no one inside the outpost willing to cross the few yards of open
ground to the helicopter. After a few minutes, he lifted out and gunships
were called in to destroy the ammunition he had left beside the outpost.

[6] A favorite district ploy had a company of RF moving out from the dis-

Not once in 1967 did a Sector or District operation in Vinh Long continue overnight. Here is how one of these operations went:

The troop left the Caumoy Bridge at 8:00 A.M. and moved in river assault (RAG) boats about two miles up the Mang Thit Canal to an outpost. They debarked and cut inland while their commander, a major from Province headquarters, installed himself in the outpost.

The troops were closing on a tree line 1000 yards due east of the outpost when they ran into snipers. We could see it all from the outpost. After an excited discussion via radio, the major announced to his American adviser that the advancing units had flushed a company of Viet Cong. He asked for helicopter gunships. The adviser, a young captain, climbed onto the outpost roof for a better look. Every few minutes there would be a snap-snap sound from the tree line, followed by a roar of semi-automatic and automatic weapons fire from the Vietnamese troops strung out along dikes in the paddy. The major's men did not appear to be availing themselves of the several excellent, heavily wooded infiltration routes that led from the dikes into the enemy-occupied tree line.

"I think maybe we wait," the young captain said. "Maybe you tell your men look for VC little bit. Then we call helicopters."

"Okay, I tell them," the Vietnamese major said gravely.

The captain installed his radio on the roof and waited. The snap snap — roar, snap snap — roar continued to echo intermittently in the hot damp air as the captain drifted into that compromise state of somnolence learned during nine

trict town, picking up a platoon from an outpost along the line of march, while a platoon from another outpost farther on set up a blocking position. The main force would march to the blocking position, then all units would return home in time for dinner.

months in the Delta: awake enough to hear the radio, asleep enough to dream he was somewhere else.

"Captain?" It was the Vietnamese major.

"Yes sir?"

"Beaucoup VC, captain." The major looked extremely concerned. He rubbed his chin. "I think now maybe *two* companies VC."

"Two companies," the sun-drugged captain repeated. He looked across the paddy. The scene had not changed, though he had been on the roof for an hour.

"I think maybe we call helicopters," the captain said.

The major nodded and his air of gravity deepened appropriately.

The captain had concluded that if he did not call helicopters the major's troops would spend the day at that dike line and he, the captain, might get blamed for it. Once the helicopters appeared on the horizon the VC would fade away, of course, but that at least would get the troops *moving*. The reasoning was good as far as it went and — in fairness to the captain, a good soldier — it was not his responsibility to carry it further.

A pair of gunships arrived in a half-hour and the outpost became crowded with spectators for the rocket and machine gun matinee. Finally, toward 1:00 P.M., the major announced that his men had occupied the tree line, whereupon we all sat down for a picnic lunch of fish, chicken, lobster, steamed rice, all kinds of fresh fruit and vegetables, including pineapple, and beer and rice wine. The major grew more expansive as the meal progressed, and afterward he proposed many toasts to "friendship," "We kill beaucoup VC today," "Tonight we look for Tiger, Ha! Ha!" (Tiger was a popular Vinh Long bar girl.) And so forth.

"We" did not kill beaucoup VC that day. The gunships had scared off the snipers, and at 4:00 P.M. the troops filed back to the debarkation point. One of the last men to depart stepped on a pressure mine planted by the Viet Cong. His left leg was blown off and he died. Ten others were wounded by the explosion.

This operation was "typical" in some respects, "untypical" in others. From my experience, it belongs in the lower middle over-all. They got worse. I went on one District operation that *ended* in time for breakfast. We started at 6:30 A.M. and were back in the district town, ordering Chinese soup at the marketplace, by 9:00 A.M. Apparently (he didn't say), this District Chief felt obligated to conduct an operation for the record; it had been a while since the last one.[7]

So it went in Vinh Long. GVN operated by day and the Viet Cong by night. At the morning briefing one learned what the Viet Cong had accomplished overnight, at the evening briefing one learned what RF/PF had pulled off between breakfast and dinner. Two or three times a month, troops from ARVN 9th Division moved into some part of the province in the morning. Cannon boomed, fighter-bombers and helicopters turned in the sky. All of us, even the doubters, felt the excitement. There was so much *movement*. A few hours later, as suddenly as it had started, the activity stopped. The troops and planes and generals went home to dinner.

Meanwhile, the outposts persisted — undefeated, never defeating, tying down 80 percent of the forces in the province, the rest moving across the landscape by day, giving way to the Viet Cong at night, returning the next day, back and forth, back and forth. And backgrounding it all, the monotonous soothing rhythm of the radio — the persistence strategy put to music.

[7] Nuances like this never show up in the statistical record where one operation is as good as any other for measuring offensive drive.

"Muggy stages four four, this is Able Lakes two five, over."
"Two five, this is four four, over."
"This is two five. Outpost under attack vicinity whisky sierra two four seven three zero six; eight rounds sixty mike mike mortar, automatic weapons, request spooky, over."
"Two two, this is four four. Roger that. Any whisky india alpha, over."
"This is four four. Negative at this time. Will keep you informed, over."
"This is two two. Roger, out . . ."

II

The Web Tightens

1967: January, February, March, April, May, June . . . Viet Cong "incidents" followed one another, rhythmically, and the temptation was to ride with them, to take them as expressions of a compulsive strategy and to respond to each one as if it were merely an isolated event. This in fact is what happened and what continued to happen even after the rhythm underwent a subtle but disconcerting change. The first indications came in the October intelligence reports. Viet Cong were sighted in large numbers in places where they had not been sighted before. Intelligence rates its sources A, B, and C, according to reliability. The new enemy sightings fell into the C category, but they were made impressive by their number and consistency. Late in October, the Vinh Long S-2 (Intelligence) adviser, summarizing his daily report, cautiously suggested that the Viet Cong 306th

Main Force Battalion might have shifted its base of operations westward toward the province capital.[8]

In November, the unexplained shift in rhythm spread to
Cho Lach, a district northeast of Vinh Long city that had
been considered relatively secure. From July to November,
the Viet Cong struck at only one outpost in Cho Lach. At
2:00 A.M. on November 6, Viet Cong snipers harassed two
Cho Lach outposts. At 10:30 A.M., a time when the Viet
Cong usually stay out of sight, they hit another outpost. At
1:00 P.M., another. At 6:00 P.M., another. At 7:00 P.M., two
more. At 9:30 P.M., another. At 2:00 A.M., on November 7,
exactly twenty-four hours after it began, the rash of attacks
ended with a burst of fire directed at one more outpost, making nine altogether. In each case the firing was light. None
of the defenders was wounded. It made no sense.

On November 5, at a point eight miles southeast of Vinh
Long city and a half mile west of Route 7A, the trunk road
leading from the province capital to the Mang Thit pacification area, an outpost was overrun and its nine defenders
killed.

On November 11, a helicopter overflying National Route
4, the Delta's principal north-south highway, was downed by
.50-caliber machine gun fire at a point five miles southwest
of Vinh Long city. On November 12, 16, 20, and 24, helicopters reported receiving automatic weapons fire from the same
general area.

On November 19, at 6:50 P.M., a truck traveling north on

[8] No one can fault the S-2 for failing to tie the move with an innocuous
item in a captured Viet Cong document that had been circulating among
members of the Minh Duc DCU in October. The document listed the
priorities for Minh Duc district in the months ahead. These included the
usual disrupting of pacification, strengthening of guerrilla forces, etc. The
item in question, one of the priorities, was a cryptic urging to develop the
"City Movement" and to unite the "City Movement" with the "Total
Movement." City Movement . . . Total Movement . . . it all sounded like
more exhortive Communist jargon.

Route 4 was ambushed a mile south of where the helicopter went down; the driver was killed, the truck destroyed.

Meanwhile, traffic on Route 168 was halted altogether. This road led from Tam Binh district town to Route 7A and on into Vinh Long city. In early November, an armed convoy set out from Tam Binh to resupply outposts along Route 168. They were repulsed by Viet Cong fire. They tried again another day. Again they were driven back. They made it the third time. But for all intents and purposes Route 168 was closed off and Tam Binh was isolated on the ground.

On November 26, eight .81-mm. mortar rounds landed inside the Vinh Long airfield perimeter, causing no damage. The airfield is located on the western edge of the province capital.

On November 30, Tam Binh district town was mortared. One killed, twelve wounded.

With December came a new rush of reports of enemy movement, now in the Ba Cang area and the southern edge of Chau Thanh district which includes the province capital. These reportedly were elements of the Viet Cong 306th Battalion and possibly another unit from outside the province. The name of this new unit (if it was a new unit) and its intentions were unknown.

Shortly after midnight on December 2, a government patrol working just off the edge of the airfield runway was ambushed by Viet Cong: Five killed, three wounded.

On December 4, an outpost near Route 7A that had been overrun sixty days earlier (ten defenders and nine dependents killed), then rebuilt and restaffed, was hit again.

On December 6, after thirty days of calm, Cho Lach erupted once more. Again, nine outposts were hit. This time two of them were overrun.

On December 20, Viet Cong set up a roadblock within

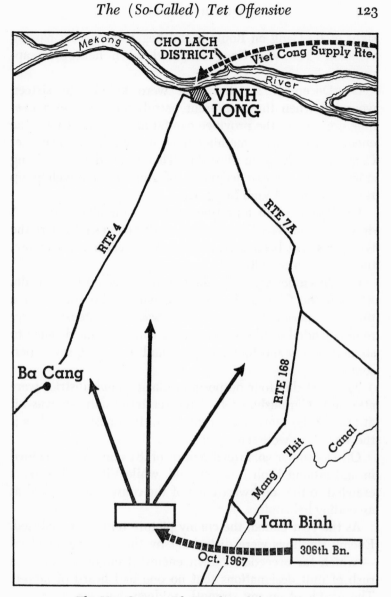

The Viet Cong 306th Battalion shifts position

sight of Ba Cang on Route 4 and began inspecting passing vehicles. The Viet Cong scattered when helicopters appeared.

On December 23, ten men were killed and sixteen wounded when three different patrols operating in a five-mile arc around the province capital made contact with the enemy. This was something new and ominous. The Viet Cong definitely were close in. That same day Viet Cong snipers fired on two jeeploads of Americans traveling up Route 7A toward Vinh Long city.

On December 26, a routine patrol moving along Route 7A drew fire from Viet Cong snipers at the same spot where the two jeeps had been fired at three days earlier. As before, there were no casualties.

On December 27, Vinh Long airfield was mortared again. As with the Cho Lach incidents, which also bracketed a thirty-day period, the second wave was more intense. Thirty rounds landed inside the perimeter causing light damage to six helicopters and four buildings and wounding seven personnel.

The next day four outposts in Chau Thanh district were attacked. Curiously, each of the scattered outposts was hit at exactly the same time: 11:45 P.M. It almost seemed as if the Viet Cong were rehearsing.

On December 30, fifteen rounds of .81-mm. mortar landed in and around Vinh Long airfield, while Viet Cong snipers crawled to the southwest edge of the runway and potted at ascending helicopters.

As the year ended, the enemy picture remained confused. Enemy sightings were disturbing by the numbers involved — which far exceeded known enemy strength — and by a rush of unit designations that no one had heard of before. The center of enemy strength, midway between Ba Cang, Tam Binh, and Vinh Long city, gave them potential to strike any of these three population centers. During the past sixty days, Vinh Long airfield had been mortared three times, Tam Binh once, and Ba Cang twice. In his year-end summary, the S-2 adviser reported that 306th Battalion, the key unit in the enemy's order of battle, appeared to be well equipped, well trained, of high morale, with a strength possibly as high as 1200 men, or three times its number on Easter Sunday.[9]

On January 1, 1968, a family of peasants at work in a rice paddy suddenly felt the earth vibrating under them. Next came a rumble that turned into a roar as two bright orange fireballs blossomed out of a tree line several hundred yards off, then billows of smoke that curled skyward 150 feet, then silence. The incident, never explained, occurred in enigmatic Cho Lach, less than three miles from the district town.

In the early morning of January 6, the Province Chief, the deputy senior U.S. adviser, and their staffs drove down Route 7A to the Caumoy Bridge to direct a Sector operation. It turned out to be the most successful such enterprise in many months — sixteen Viet Cong killed. The members of the command post element were in high spirits when, at 5:00 P.M., they began the twelve-mile drive back to Vinh Long, the Province Chief's jeep in the lead, followed by his armored car escort, then two jeeploads of Americans — the deputy senior adviser, the S-3 (Operations), S-2, and three sergeants. As usual, the Province Chief's wild driver sped off down the twisting, rutted two-lane "highway." The armored car driver maintained the pace, but the Americans, again as usual, allowed themselves to be distanced.

Halfway to Vinh Long, the lead American jeep was hit broadside by a B-40 rocket fired at pointblank range. The second jeep, two hundred yards back, halted. Someone man-

[9] I am only listing highlights. In November and December a total of 296 Viet Cong-initiated incidents were recorded in Vinh Long.

aged to get on the radio and say, "We are being hit . . . hard . . ." Captain Cline Preble, orbiting the Mang Thit in a spotter plane, heard the transmission. Knowing the command unit was proceeding up Route 7A, Preble headed that way in a hurry. When he arrived overhead, less than two minutes later, it was all over. He could see the jeeps in the road, smoking, flame buds licking the paint off one of them, and around the jeeps, scattered like dolls, the bodies. Preble immediately came under fire from .30- and .50-caliber machine guns installed in a tree line paralleling the road. He radioed for helicopter gunships. In the engagement that developed, the Province Chief and his deputy were wounded. The Viet Cong broke contact at about 9:00 P.M. and faded away. They left no bodies. By guerrilla warfare standards, they had committed the perfect crime. Not one member of the U.S. command element survived.

There was of course an investigation and a report. After all, Route 7A was: "Secure." The population: "Friendly." The briefing charts said so. The investigation showed that two hundred Viet Cong set up machine gun and rocket positions along the road in the morning and waited among the friendly population until the returning convoy passed their way at dusk. They had the area superbly reconnoitered. They even had tested their plan: It was on this same spot that our units received fire on December 23 and December 26. The purpose of these isolated incidents now became clear. The identity of the guilty party was no less obvious: the Viet Cong 306th Battalion. In his summary of that day's activities, meant for his superiors at Division and Corps, a grieving deputy S-2 adviser delivered a request almost pathetic for its chances. Would it be possible, he inquired, for ARVN 9th Division, with all its mobility and fire support, to conduct an operation of several days' duration against units of the Viet Cong 306th Battalion? The 306th presented a "persistent threat" to Vinh Long, it was capable of striking "any target" in the province, and its area of operations had been moved dangerously close to the province capital. Naturally, an operation of several days' duration was out of the question. The longest 9th Division operation in anyone's memory ran forty-eight hours. Besides, why all the fuss about the 306th Battalion?

> "Since Easter, the 306th [has] broken up into small units . . . We have obviously gained the upper hand over the 306th Main Force Battalion."
>
> Brigadier General William Desobry
> January 9, 1968
> (Three days *after* the ambush in Vinh Long.)

In Vinh Long, they knew better. If anyone had the "upper hand" it was the 306th. After the ambush, an order went out to American personnel declaring Route 7A off limits to all but armed convoy traffic cleared at the TOC.[10]

First, the Ba Ke road (Route 168) leading into Route 7A, now Route 7A itself. And:

On January 16, Viet Cong hit Ba Cang on Route 4 for the second time in two weeks. During the previous sixty days, twenty-one Viet Cong initiated incidents had been recorded for the ten-mile stretch of road between Ba Cang and Vinh Long city; that is exclusive of attacks on nearby outposts and ground fire directed at helicopters. Clearly, Route 4 was not "secure" either. The web was tightening.

On January 20, a USAID interpreter mentioned in conversation with an American that his home was now filled with relatives from a village two miles south of Vinh Long city.

---

[10] This was a major defeat. Route 7A was the principal land line to the number one priority pacification project in the entire Delta. I had driven it unescorted dozens of times.

They were visiting, he said, because Viet Cong had occupied their village.

On January 27, Viet Cong cadre passed through a hamlet bordering the province capital and distributed leaflets saying they would be using the area for a while, that all inhabitants should leave, and that anyone who went to the authorities would be decapitated.

By now, the flow of intelligence had become a flood. Viet Cong were everywhere. The ARVN S-2 reported that the Viet Cong commissar for Chau Thanh district surrounding the province capital had ordered all inhabitants to remain in their homes between the hours of 6:00 P.M. and 7:00 A.M.

Vinh Long province headquarters, 9th Division headquarters, IV Corps headquarters knew an attack of some sort was imminent, but they didn't do anything. They just stood there, before those soothing wall maps and briefing charts, and waited.

III

Attack

The traditional three-day Tet Lunar New Year truce, honored by GVN and Viet Cong, began this year on January 29, the holiday itself the evening of the thirtieth. Everywhere the mood was festive. In Vinh Long, municipal loudspeakers blared music, and banners hung from buildings and over the crowded streets.

At 9:45 A.M. on January 30, a cryptic order came down from 9th Division headquarters stating that the Tet truce was cancelled forthwith. Provincial officials filed the order and went on celebrating. So far, the Viet Cong had observed the truce to the letter. The preceding night, for the first time in weeks, the enemy had not provoked a single incident. The consensus seemed to be that they weren't about to start on the first feast night.

The Americans, most of whom were experiencing their first Tet, followed the Vietnamese lead. Captain John Graham, the new S-2 adviser, and his deputy, Lieutenant John Lippincott, were guests at the home of their interpreter. The feast began at 3:00 P.M. with a variety of Vietnamese hors d'oeuvres to be washed down with rice wine (a potent beverage) and/or Scotch whisky (somewhat milder). Lieutenant Lippincott was just beginning to unwind from the tensions of past weeks when a messenger came by to advise him that he was night duty officer at the TOC. No, that's tomorrow night, Lippincott said. But he had misread the roster. Reluctantly, the young lieutenant returned home, changed his civilian clothes for olive fatigues, and drove across town to the TOC. There the day officer briefed him and left. Still feeling the rice wine, Lippincott stretched out on a cot and dropped off to sleep.

When he awoke, it was dark. Ten o'clock. Lippincott moved over to a chair by the radio, lit his pipe, and began thumbing through a magazine.

A voice broke through the radio static. It was Vung Liem, reporting harassment of an outpost, the first incident of any kind in two days. Lippincott noted the time in his log — 12:30 A.M. — and resumed reading. Shortly before 3:00 A.M., the telephone rang. It was Lieutenant Colonel Roberge, senior provincial adviser, calling from the MACV house (the advisory team billet). What was that noise at the airfield? Lippincott had heard nothing. He ordered his radio operator to call the control tower, and he stepped outside. Standing there in the quiet courtyard Lippincott detected a distant thumping sound. He reentered the TOC in time to hear the control tower report: "We are under heavy mortar attack." As he passed the information to Roberge on the telephone, Vung Liem subsector reported they were under attack. Lippincott passed this on. Then machine gun and rifle fire broke out all around him.

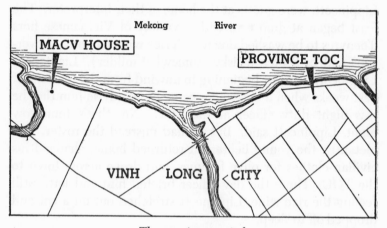

The province capital

John Graham, the S-2, had drawn a helicopter "firefly" mission that night.[11] The mission was to run from 11:00 P.M. to 4:00 A.M., but when the three ships put down for refueling at 2:45 A.M. Graham and the pilots had all but decided to remain on the ground. They couldn't see any point continuing: It was too quiet. Incoming mortars changed all that. As they scrambled aloft they could see tracers headed their way

[11] The "firefly" is a helicopter that skims over suspected Viet Cong areas, landing lights aglow. If it draws fire, two gunships circling much higher swoop down and open up with rockets and machine guns.

from positions around the airfield. The Viet Cong were moving in on the ground, too.

John Graham crouched by the circling helicopter's open doorway, through which, at intervals, the crew chief was hurling flares. Graham couldn't believe it. Five minutes earlier the province capital had been like a graveyard. Now: Muzzle flashes everywhere, explosions, small fires starting . . .

John Lippincott felt as if he were dreaming, seeing himself in the dream. He was in a building, the TOC, in Vinh Long; the place had been transformed into a madhouse, and the inmates were running berserk in the middle of the night. He moved among them but they did not see him. He talked to them but they did not answer. Only the radio was real. He talked calmly on the radio. Then he walked with his interpreter to where the senior Vietnamese officer (a colonel) was standing: "Helicopter pilots are receiving intense fire from these coordinates, sir." He read them. "Should they return fire?" The Vietnamese colonel made no reply. He looked at Lippincott but gave no sign of recognition. Lippincott walked back to the radio. Now Roberge had a question. "Yes sir, I'll ask him." Lippincott walked among the desks to where the colonel was standing. He asked the question. Again the glassy stare. Again the walk back. "Are the Rangers committed yet?" (ARVN 9th Division had ordered Province to commit the elite ARVN 43rd Ranger Battalion quartered on the edge of the city). "I don't know sir, I'll ask." Lippincott walked and saw himself walking. "Excuse me, Colonel. Are the Rangers committed yet?" Lippincott waited and looked into the glassy eyes until he became uncomfortable, but he returned later, and again, and again, through the night.

The Vietnamese command center was simply immobilized; they had gone into shock. Their occasional orders showed no discernible pattern. The situation was not fluid (in the military sense) so much as it was disjointed. The ARVN 3/2 Armored Cav troop had moved into the city, somewhere. RAG gunboats were on station offshore, directing .20- and .40-mm. cannon and .50-caliber machine gun fire and mortars into the city. (The Cav and the RAG boats were out of sight of each other and at one point they got involved in a thunderous duel that took off part of the roof of the TOC.)

Still no word on the Rangers.

Later, as it became evident the Viet Cong had neither the desire nor the firepower to storm the TOC compound, some of the shock began to wear off. The Vietnamese colonel walked up to Lippincott. "VC plan number ten," he blustered. (Number ten is pigeon for very bad.) "Cannot take city. Number ten plan. With one hundred men, I take whole city." "Yes sir," Lippincott said. "You take whole city. Yes, yes." The colonel laughed boisterously.

A team of American advisers headed by Roberge made it to the TOC by RAG boat on the afternoon of the first day. But the government response, over which the Americans exercised little control, remained as confused as ever. None of the advisers was sure what was happening outside the TOC compound. The Cav were out there, and the ARVN Rangers (who had moved out, finally, at 9:00 A.M.), and the Viet Cong, and they were all making a racket, but to what end no one could be really sure.

The fighting continued through the day, the night, and into the next morning. Then, at noon, everything stopped. The city turned quiet.

The silence was, in its suddenness, as bewildering as the attack. The Americans waited expectantly. Nothing happened. Apparently, it was all over. The strategy of confusion had worked, Lord only knows how.

"Four four, this is eight eight, four four this is eight eight."
The adviser to the Rangers: *"This is eight eight, go ahead."*

The message came over garbled. Something like *"Unit running loose . . . looting . . . separated from my counterpart . . ."*

A few minutes later, the report was confirmed by another Ranger adviser. The Viet Cong had withdrawn. Most of the local inhabitants had fled during the battle. That left the city to the ARVN Rangers and they were breaking into shops and homes, taking everything they could carry.

The Rangers, joined later by elements of the Cav, looted through the day, slept that night, and resumed looting the next morning, and continued looting until the Viet Cong resurfaced in the early afternoon.[12] That brought back gunships with their rockets and machine guns and RAG boats with their cannon and mortars.

When, by evening, the situation had not improved, it was decided that U.S. civilian AID workers should be evacuated by boat down the Bassac River to the U.S. 9th Division base camp in Dong Tam. The AID workers began their journey late at night aboard an LCM. As the boat moved southward past the city, they stood at the rail and stared in horror and disbelief. Helicopter gunships hovered about, sending down tracers in red streams and rockets that exploded on impact. Flares drifted down into the billowing smoke and mixed with flames from burning buildings to tint the moonless sky an eerie orange. A spasmodic boom boom boom — like a bass drum — issued from the rapid-fire cannon of the RAG boats gliding back and forth in the river opposite the flaming city.

The battle raged for two more days and nights without noticeable progress either way. On February 5, 1000 U.S.

---

[12] Cav advisers deny their unit participated in the looting. But I interviewed several witnesses, including one American, who testified to the contrary.

troops were committed and, finally, on February 6, the Viet Cong were driven out. The next day U.S. forces withdrew, and ARVN units established a defense perimeter.

Refugees came filtering back into the smoking city, down roads and across bridges by which the Viet Cong had entered and left. They wandered past bodies decaying in the hot sun, past blown-out armored cars. They found some streets untouched, others leveled. One hundred dead civilians were pulled out of the rubble. Fourteen hundred more had been wounded. A total of 15,000 (out of a population of 40,000) had been made homeless. But statistics — and there would be plenty of statistics — tell only part of the story. In the aftermath, the essential fact was this: During two decades of war, the Viet Cong had never before invaded Vinh Long city.

IV

The Veil Lifts

Initially, in their public and private assessments of the Tet Offensive, American officials were frankly pessimistic. But just as it appeared they might be on the verge of a soul-searching examination into the root causes of U.S.-GVN weakness, a correction set in. The impact of the offensive, U.S. officials said, was not as bad as first believed. The Viet Cong had not captured a single province capital. Not a single ARVN unit had gone over to the enemy. On the other hand, Viet Cong losses were enormous. In the Delta: 6500 killed, an estimated three times that many wounded, meaning at least one-fourth of all Viet Cong guerrilla and main force personnel had been put out of action, etc.

To understand how the Tet Offensive happened, and why, it is necessary to do what our officials did not do. It is necessary to broaden the perspective and examine the Tet Offensive for what it was — not a classic collision of forces that can be machine-graded as "winners" or "losers," but one more violent pulsation from the Viet Cong web, the Easter Sunday battle on a much grander scale. As with the battle, any meaningful assessment must begin with an appraisal of the offensive's impact on the system itself: Did we profit from the experience? If we did not profit, then we lost — in the same way that a man who has suffered a heart attack loses when he does not take corrective measures to prevent another, but instead pronounces himself fit as ever, using as evidence the incontrovertible fact that he did not die.

The events of January 31–February 5 were, most of all, an unveiling. The Viet Cong unveiling came when they surfaced to attack; it was strategic. Our unveiling was psychological. It came with the disruption of a working compromise with reality. The Viet Cong increased the pressure until the compromise exploded. Puff.

It is now clear that the Tet attacks were only the high point in a carefully orchestrated offensive that had been under way for several months without U.S.-GVN even knowing it. The primary objective was Vinh Long city and the strategy was to move in strength closer and closer around the city, interrupt GVN land lines of communication, and secure Viet Cong supply lines for the big assault. Secondary objectives were the district towns, each of which met with a miniaturized version of the developing assault on Vinh Long city. For the attack on the province capital, the coordinating unit was the 306th Battalion: the DCUs had responsibility for the district towns.[13]

The offensive got under way in the early fall of 1967 when the 306th Battalion shifted west of the Mang Thit canal. Prior to the shift, the main Viet Cong thrust was against the Mang Thit pacification project. After the shift, it seemed vaguely directed over a broad area. Our intelligence could not grasp the new matrix; as a consequence, Viet Cong incidents and activity no longer made sense. "Sometime in the fall," a Vinh Long intelligence officer told me with commendable frankness, "we lost our picture of the VC."

Pressures against the district towns increased the mystery by dispersing the threat. Unlike the province capital, which was never menaced directly until the main assault, most of the district towns came under mortar attack in December and January. By mid-January, Tam Binh was effectively cut off by road from the province capital, Ba Cang was under continuous pressure, the Vung Liem and Tra On district chiefs had stopped operating outside their district towns, and something strange was going on in Cho Lach.

The Cho Lach incidents, by the way, were tied in with Viet Cong supply movements. MACV assertions about supplies from Cambodia notwithstanding, the principal supply routes for Vinh Long province flowed from south to north and, in particular, from east to west. The latter route originated in the mangrove swamps in Vinh Binh and Kien Hoa provinces along the South China Sea. The supplies moved westward into Cho Lach, then down into Vinh Long city itself where they were buried in graveyards, under bridges, and even inside flower pots.[14] The mysterious explosion near

[13] One exception was Minh Duc district. The Minh Duc DCU was diverted to help in the attack on Vinh Long city.
[14] After the offensive, Vinh Long police uncovered a weapons cache under a bridge in the province capital. They found: 2 RQG 7 rockets, 21 B-40

Cho Lach district town probably was a load of ammunition bound for the province capital.

By December, Viet Cong were all over Chau Thanh district, though to no apparent purpose. That they were swinging in an ever-tightening arc from Ba Cang on Route 4 to Route 7A did not become apparent until mid-January, and when it became apparent, no one acted.

In sum, the Viet Cong held the offensive in Vinh Long for four months right up to the Tet attack. It was an extraordinary performance. Even now, with all the benefits of hindsight, it requires a special effort of the imagination to picture the bustle of Viet Cong activity from November through January, especially the flow of men and supplies, all concealed as effectively as if the web had dropped ten feet under ground and was spreading out under the city itself.

The man ultimately responsible for ARVN actions during this period was the 9th Division Commander, General Thi. Through January, despite entreaties from Vinh Long advisers, despite the disastrous ambush on Route 7A, Thi permitted only two typically inconclusive 8:00 A.M. to 4:00 P.M. division operations near the 306th Battalion staging area in Vinh Long. Thi's unveiling came with the big attack when his strategy of persistence showed up under pressure as the strategy of paralysis.

At the height of the attacks, on February 2, three American civilians, a young man and two girls who had sought refuge at the ARVN 9th Division headquarters compound in Sadec, found themselves confronted by an ARVN officer. The general cordially invites you to tea, the officer said. The three Americans gratefully accepted. They were anxious to

---

rockets, 3 rds. .75 mm. recoilless rifle, 40 shoebox-type mines, 6 anti-tank mines, 30 boxes of small arms ammunition and several hand grenades. All these items were smuggled in, one at a time presumably, collected and buried.

find out how the battle was going. The officer led them up the stone staircase and along the colonnaded balcony (an inheritance of the Golden Age of France) past the crowded Division TOC, where the visitors had expected to find the general, and into Thi's private office where they did find him, alone, seated at his desk, gazing off into space. Ah my American friends, the general said. Please sit down. Please join me for tea. An aide poured. The gracious general chatted about this and that. At one point, he volunteered that he had studied philosophy. At the famous Sorbonne in Paris. He wrote his thesis on Kant. One of the Americans admired Sartre. *Bien sur que Sartre a quelque chose à dire, mais* . . . Thi had read *Being and Nothingness* and found it a bit foggy. For that genre he preferred Heidegger. Finally one of the Americans could stand it no longer. "What is going to happen, General?" he blurted. Happen? Happen? *Eh bien* . . . Thi paused and gazed off into space. When he spoke again, it was as if to himself. "If they succeed, they succeed," he said, with a shrug, "and if they fail they fail." [15] It was out of his hands. Such was the mood of El Supremo at the height of the Tet Offensive.

In the days after the attack the "persistence" and "victory" strategies collided in full view. The Americans said, "They've fled. Let's go get them." ARVN said, "Let's wait and see." The result: Americans fretted, ARVN waited. U.S. intelligence officers had the Viet Cong base camp areas located to their satisfaction, but ARVN refused to move out from the city more than a mile or two. Instead, they requested air strikes in the enemy's general direction. This fundamental difference in attitude between ARVN and their advisers surfaced dramatically during a brief exchange be-

[15] Thi used the Vietnamese expression *"Neu thang thi thang, neu thua thi thua."*

tween the senior adviser and his acting Vietnamese counterpart while on an inspection tour by helicopter (no roads
were safe) of the province. They were at the district chief's
headquarters in Vung Liem.[16] "Now," said the Vietnamese
colonel, "we talk about plan to defend . . ." The American's
interruption came like a whip crack. "You mean plan to attack . . ."

Meanwhile, GVN civilian officials calmly reoccupied the
province headquarters and took the dozen safes the ARVN
Rangers had blown open and emptied and stacked them outside where they remained for several days, a symbol of law-
lessness, but — ironically — only to the Americans. The
Vietnamese cared less. They were not accountable for looted
funds, even though the looters were, technically, their subordinates. As for the damages, they simply drew up a list of
expenses for repairs. The list was forwarded to Saigon for
action ultimately, by the Americans who could not say no.
Reconstruction would be handled by Vinh Long contrac-
tors, with province officials taking the usual rake-off. To the
GVN civilian persistence strategists the lesson learned from
the attack was that even in destruction there were profits, so
long as the high-spending American advisers could be kept
fretting about "rapport." The list of reconstruction expenses
included 1,500,000 piastres for a province judge's home,
400,000 for the prosecutor's home, 400,000 for the home of
the deputy province chief for security ("now we talk about
plan to defend . . ."), and 600,000 for the deputy province
chief for administration.

The main thrust of the post-Tet U.S. civilian effort went
toward reconstruction. Americans respond outstandingly to
disasters, partly, I think, because disaster relief has been
sanctified in the American ethic: Our belief in building-as-
progress, with its moral implications of salvation through

[16] I happened to be already there visiting.

hard work, reaches the summit of fulfillment in disaster relief. In Vinh Long, after the Tet Offensive, American civilian advisers threw themselves into disaster relief with visible mental relief. For once in this shadowy war, the requirements for doing good were obvious and attainable, and the results promised to be *visual*. Thus "progress" would be recorded honestly as, week by week, X amount of food was distributed and Y amount of roofs were made available. I don't mean to be cynical. Americans *were* doing good. What made the process fascinating was its glaring contrast to past efforts where goals were less clear-cut. I recall the performance of one AID worker in particular, a former Peace Corpsman in South America. He worked day and night. It was as if the challenge had released vast stores of energy. By his actions he seemed to be saying, "This is what I came here for, to help suffering people; if only it all could be this simple."

But it wasn't, and wouldn't be. On February 9, Hugh Lobit, a civilian AID worker, ventured a half mile outside Vinh Long city to inspect a "pacified" hamlet. A few hours later, a search party found him lying on a road in the hamlet with a bullet in his brain. The Viet Cong were still in tight. Within a few days, they had begun filtering back into town. Another AID worker was advised by Vietnamese friends to stop visiting the city's main refugee camp, located on the sprawling grounds of a Catholic church. The Viet Cong had infiltrated the camp, he was told. The American reported this intelligence to Vietnamese authorities, but no action was taken.

Finally, on February 18, the Viet Cong attacked again. The scale was smaller, the response better coordinated, and the damage considerably less.

But the attack left its mark. No one who witnessed it is

likely to forget what happened that afternoon. The MACV house was taking sniper fire. Americans responded with machine guns and M-16s from positions along the balconies on each floor of their five-story concrete billet. Suddenly the shooting stopped. The Americans crouched and waited uneasily. Last time, silence had been a prelude to mass looting.

"What's that?"

"Where?"

"Down the road. Something moving."

The men waited, and watched, and, slowly, one by one, they stood up.

The MACV house was situated on the edge of town on the road to Sadec. Now, moving out from the center, down that road, came the citizens of Vinh Long, on foot, some carrying bundles, others pushing loaded carts. Apparently, some sort of truce had been arranged to empty out the refugee camps that the Viet Cong, as the U.S. civilian had warned, were using as staging areas for their attacks.

And so we stood there on the balconies for more than an hour as they passed beneath us, thousands of tired people marching silently down the road with their bundles, behind them smoke curling over the city. Some Americans felt the irony. First the Viet Cong occupied the surrounding countryside, forcing the people into the city. Then the Viet Cong occupied the city, and U.S.-ARVN leveled blocks and blocks, forcing half the population into refugee camps. Now the Viet Cong occupied the refugee camps, and the people were fleeing the city for the countryside that the government had abandoned in order to better protect the city. Did the people hate the Viet Cong? Maybe. But in whom had they confidence? Not in the government. Not now. Not with their homes destroyed by U.S. aircraft and looted by government troops, and their remaining sanctuary unsafe from Viet Cong infiltration.

The last refugees passed on down the road and out of sight, the Americans crouched behind balcony walls, and, as if on signal from some unseen director, the firing resumed. But it was different now. Viet Cong and U.S.-ARVN had become performers without an audience. Not long after the exodus of refugees the Viet Cong withdrew.

An exodus of a different sort took place February 21. That morning several hundred local residents converged on the RAG base in Vinh Long city. Men in custom-tailored suits, women in exquisite ao dais, they mingled in little groups; the women twirled colorful umbrellas. To the American RAG advisers, it looked like a misplaced lawn party. The RAG commander would not say who the people were. He seemed irritated by their presence. Toward noon, the commander ushered his guests into landing craft and took them to meet a freighter that had appeared on the horizon. Where are they going, the Americans asked the sullen commander after he returned. He said only, "To Saigon." Further inquiries shed some light on the mystery ship and its plush cargo. Officially, the ship had been sent down from Saigon to collect civil servants visiting relatives for Tet and stranded by the Viet Cong attack. It appeared, however, that the civil servant crowd was heavily infiltrated by local notables anxious to get out while they could and willing to pay a high price for the privilege.

After inspecting the damage caused by air-ground "defense" of the city, the U.S. senior adviser issued a firm order that henceforth under no circumstances would air power be called in within the city limits.[17] ARVN would drive out the

17 In all fairness, the air-strikes problem was more complicated than some press reports made it. The greatest damage appears to have been the result of a not unusual — for the circumstances — authorization for helicopter gunships to respond to "intensive" ground fire. When the authorization was granted, the city was infested with Viet Cong; for all anyone knew the

Viet Cong on the ground, he said, or they would not be driven out at all. In other words, the Americans had learned from the experience. Had ARVN?

One can only speculate how Thi and his unit commanders felt about the destruction, but in the days following the Viet Cong withdrawal, they gave no indication they were prepared to put into effect the only sensible strategy open to them, which was to keep the enemy out of the city, to pursue the enemy rather than wait for him to strike again. When, to no one's surprise, the Viet Cong did strike again, ARVN commanders reverted to their old habits of calling for air strikes as a substitute for — not in support of — maneuver on the ground. On February 18, for example, I happened to monitor a radio conversation between the TOC duty officer in Vinh Long and the adviser to a battalion protecting the city. Viet Cong were filtering into the city between two of the battalion's companies and the battalion commander asked his American adviser to request an air strike.

"Are there friendly structures in the target area?" the TOC officer inquired.

"Affirmative."

"What is the distance between friendly units?"

"About three hundred meters."

"Negative. Negative on your request. Tell counterpart no air strikes in populated areas. *Advise* him to close the gap on the ground."

This was not an isolated incident. Other requests to shell houses were denied. ARVN just wouldn't learn — or didn't

---

TOC might be overrun at any minute; ARVN officers in the TOC had slipped into a state of shock; the city's only maneuver element was bottled up, then fighting, then running amuck. The gunship pilots, for their part, felt angry and frightened: The airfield was under ground attack; the airfield commander was dead, as were many of their buddies. Not surprisingly, they responded with fury.

care. The evidence suggests to me that ARVN — more specifically, ARVN commanders — didn't care.

The most damning piece of evidence is this: The ARVN
9th Division unit that should have cared most for the people
of Vinh Long city because it was based in that city for more
than three years was the 43rd Rangers, the unit that looted
the city. In effect, the Rangers were looting their neighbors.
Yet no one expressed surprise at their actions. It seems that
the Rangers had been looting their neighbors, albeit less dramatically, for a long time. Ranger commanders took a percentage from the bars and had a hand in several other local
enterprises, notably a lucrative nightclub-restaurant. The
line soldiers drank in the bars without paying, beat up
people they didn't like, and committed occasional thefts; the
police — weaker in numbers and weaponry — had no choice
but to look the other way. The Americans in Vinh Long
were not happy about this situation, but their hands were
tied by sensitive senior officers in Can Tho and Saigon ob-
sessed with "rapport." There was nothing to do about these
little bandits but tolerate them — and make the best of it.

Everyone had a favorite Rangers story. Mine concerns an
event that became known in the Americans' underground
folklore as "The Battle of Vinh Long City." It happened one
evening in July 1967. The ARVN 2/2 Cav troop was bivouacked for the night on the outskirts of town. Some soldiers
from that unit were making the rounds of the local bars
when they got into a dispute with a group of Rangers. A
Ranger drew first and shot one of the Cav troopers dead.
Later that night, the Cav advisers were awakened by the
unmistakable sound of armored personnel carriers tuning up.
At 11:00 P.M.? Very unlike ARVN. The bewildered Americans got up in time to see the APCs pull out of the camp and
pivot onto the highway leading into Vinh Long city.

The lead APC caught a Ranger jeep cruising through town
and drove it into a wall. Other Rangers responded with M-

79 grenade launchers. The Cav opened up with their .30-caliber machine guns. (One can imagine a stray Viet Cong watching in wonder from behind a tree.) The local CIA representative, an American, was driving home from a movie at the MACV house. He got caught in a crossfire and rocketed up a side street, certain the Viet Cong were attacking. By the time order was restored, the toll for both sides was five dead and seven wounded. A squad of Rangers waited in ambush near the hospital part of the night in the vain hope that the Cav would bring in their casualties.[18]

Not long after the Battle of Vinh Long city, the Ranger commander, a colonel, was relieved of his post. Rumor said he was being disciplined. Not quite. He was promoted. He took over a Ranger Group in I Corps. Many observers would later hail the performance of the colonel's troops during the recapture of Hue. Could this man be both a hero and a crook? The answer is yes. For the colonel embodies a quite understandable contradiction not uncommon in the better Vietnamese officers educated by the French and trained by the Americans. The colonel's Western manners made him likable to Americans. But these same manners contributed to his attitude of superiority over most Vietnamese. He fought hard and well (in the best Hemingway tradition), yet he had no feeling for the people he was paid to defend. He killed the "enemy" and he took what he wanted from his "friends." It never occurred to him that one action cancelled out the other. He was a mercenary in his own country. And we were paying his salary.

.

[18] That evening I was visiting with Fred Abramson, an AID worker, at the U.S. civilian offices downtown. He was working late, as he often did. I was seated facing the window, and when the .30 caliber tracers shot past, I instinctively hit the deck. Fred got on the phone to TOC. "What's going on," he asked. "Oh . . . thanks . . ." He hung up. "What is it? What is it?" Fred smiled sheepishly. "Oh, hell, it's only the Rangers."

General Thi did not order the Rangers disciplined for pillaging the city. The unit was simply transferred to another city, as their former commander was transferred. When the problem becomes too obvious, it should be transferred out: This was the lesson learned from the rape of Vinh Long.

Yet despite so much evidence to the contrary the official word came to be that General Thi scored a remarkable "victory" during Tet. The veil had been lifted, his weaknesses displayed, but now it was being allowed to fall again, and as the weeks passed the delicate balance gradually was restored — on the surface.[19] Once again the great general, the hero of Easter Sunday and now of Tet, had proven the invincibility of the strategy of persistence.

The veil came down again over the countryside too. Our pacification experts put together a corrected version of events that bore the unmistakable imprint of the computer mentality: Statistics and more statistics — all accurate. The trouble was they related only incidentally to what was happening.

In arguing that the Delta countryside had not been abandoned to the Viet Cong, the pacification experts cited the fact that out of 205 pacification teams in the field before Tet, more than one-half remained on station throughout the attacks. This is interesting, but irrelevant. The pacification program is directed at only a tiny part of the countryside, less than 10 percent at any one time. The Viet Cong can dominate the countryside without touching the pacification program. In Vinh Long that is precisely what happened. During the weeks after the attack on the province capital, the Viet Cong concentrated on the district towns. They ignored the pacification hamlets almost completely. The ham-

[19] Later in 1968, Brigadier General Thi was relieved of his command. No, no, no . . . he was not reprimanded. He was promoted to Major General and named commandant of the ARVN military academy at Dalat — the Vietnamese equivalent of West Point.

lets might have seemed important to "progress"-minded Americans, but they were not important to the Viet Cong.

In the broader context of pacification-and-aid programs — public health, agricultural development, etc. — the real situation in at least one Vinh Long district was exposed as being totally at variance with the official picture. On the eve of the Tet Offensive, Cho Lach district (pop. 61,054) was the pride of the Vinh Long provincial administration. According to GVN briefing charts, thirty of the district's thirty-two hamlets were under government control; one hamlet (pop. 705) belonged to the Viet Cong, and one hamlet (pop. 564) was "contested." [20] The previous September, elections had been held in all Cho Lach's nine villages and in thirty-one hamlets, the best record in the province.[21] Government information offices were functioning without harassment in every village and in twenty-three hamlets. Twenty-three public health officers roved the district, treating an average of 3100 persons a month and sending the most serious cases to a twelve-bed infirmary installed in the district capital. The agricultural bureau had nine roving personnel in the district; they were introducing new vegetable crops and promoting a popular program to raise rabbits as a meat source. Plans for a soccer league reportedly had brought an enthusiastic response from the populace. Etc., etc. Cho Lach was going nowhere but up up up on the "progress" charts at province headquarters.

[20] U.S. briefers privately placed three more hamlets in the "contested" category. Even according to this more conservative appraisal, well over 90 percent of the population in the district belonged to the government.
[21] Under national law, elections are permitted in hamlets and villages as they become "secure," i.e., loyal to the government. The hamlet is the basic political entity. Hamlets are grouped into villages which are grouped into districts. Citizens vote for hamlet and village officers, for representatives to the National Assembly, and for President of the Republic. Province officials are appointed by the national government and district officials are appointed by province.

Three weeks after the Tet Offensive, forty-two out of fifty government outposts in the district sat empty, abandoned. The American adviser in the district reported that all thirty-two hamlets were under Viet Cong control. The government controlled only the district town. The most pacified district had become the least pacified district.

The events in Cho Lach point up a basic weakness in our measurement techniques. The Viet Cong are advancing on two fronts; one is military, the other is socio-political. The military side is handled by the Viet Cong *army;* the socio-political side is handled by the Viet Cong *organization,* consisting of hamlet, village, district, and province shadow governments, tax collectors, drama teams, youth club leaders, and so forth. Our assessment of the Viet Cong in Cho Lach was based almost exclusively on Viet Cong *military* activity which was minimal. When at the same time we had considerable statistical evidence of GVN progress we presumed the area to be pacified or on its way toward pacification. Left out of the measuring process was Cho Lach's remarkably efficient Viet Cong organization.

Not only did we not know what half the enemy were doing in Cho Lach, but we did not know much about our allies either. To admit that forty-two outposts could have been abandoned simultaneously is to admit a coincidence of inconceivable proportions, as would be also the shift in allegiance overnight of the great bulk of the district's population. In short, the extent of Viet Cong influence in Cho Lach was "unveiled" during the Tet Offensive. The unveiling could not have come as a surprise to the residents of Cho Lach since it was their condition that was exposed. Could the local officials have been totally unaware of the real situation in the district they were administering? I am one who does not believe Vietnamese officials are that stupid. I think they knew. And this is what makes the Cho Lach case so ominous. Because it would seem that the only people who did not know the extent of Viet Cong influence, who actually believed the statistics, were the Americans.

⚑

The evidence in Vinh Long suggests to me that the Vietnam "problem" was made insoluble by the early decision to operate behind a veil of Rapport and Optimism. Our hope was that we could work changes behind the veil. What happened, though, was that we got locked in. And we multiplied.

During the Tet Offensive, the veil was lifted. It came down again, hurriedly, but not before those who witnessed the event saw that nothing had changed, nothing at all.

Reflections on the Military

In watching the American military perform in the Delta, I became conscious of a gap in their ranks — a generational gap, in part particular to the war, but also related, I think, to the ability of the military institution to adapt to the requirements of the Vietnam assignment.

What was particular to the war was the insight afforded junior officers and denied generals. In Korea in the 1950s, in Europe and the Pacific in the 1940s, in Europe in 1917–18, the clearest picture of the war was obtainable at the command level. This was because the action — troop movement, territorial gains, enemy losses — offered up positive indicators of progress and this information was available only from those with a broad overview, i.e., the big-unit commanders. In the Vietnam war as often as not the reverse was true: Progress was not determined by action. You could have vast amounts of action and no progress.

The most reliable gauge of the state of the war in the Delta at any one time came, instead, from a subtle unquantifiable factor that I would call its rhythm. You did not get the rhythm by moving up to the front lines during peak moments when the enemy was engaged. You got it from staying around through the whole wearying performance — day after day, week after week, sometimes even month after month of nothing but tiny ominous pinpricks. The habit commanders had of moving in close when the shooting started and moving out when the shooting stopped was a little like trying to judge a symphony by listening only to its crescendos. Moreover, since U.S.-ARVN forces, with their superior firepower and battle maneuverability, almost invariably scored "body count" victories in head-on encounters, the picture offered big-unit commanders was one of an unbroken string of successes. The picture was accurate for the battles, it was not accurate for the war. As a result, a true picture of the war was most often available from junior officers living in the field where the daily rhythm could be felt.

Now it happened that most of those junior officers closest to the war's true picture were young men in their twenties. So you had in Vietnam a gap in information that paralleled a gap in age.

Lodged in the center of this gap, preventing it from being bridged, was a powerful institutional instrument — the annual efficiency report.[22]

Each officer is rated once a year by his immediate superior.[23] The rating goes on a permanent record that follows him onward and upward throughout his career. It is like collecting fouls in a basketball game. The men charged with evaluating an officer for promotion rely heavily on these efficiency reports. To protect his career, the young officer learns to size up his immediate superior and gear his performance to what the boss expects. The boss, for his part, has an eye on *his* superior, and on up the line.

[22] These remarks can also be applied to civilian agencies ruled by the efficiency report. The difference with the military is one of degree.
[23] If his tour runs less than a year he may be rated at the end of his tour.

The efficiency report is useful for keeping an army locked in on a hierarchically determined strategy.[24] The process breaks down and begins to look silly when that strategy is faulty in its conception. In Vietnam, junior officers in the field saw the faults but they were blocked from communicating their insights by layer upon layer of efficiency reports. A captain may agree with the criticism of a lieutenant he is rating, but what about the major who is rating the captain? And the colonel who is rating the major? The chances of valuable criticism breaking through to the top are not very good. Only the top-level strategists can institute changes, yet, in Vietnam, these same men are insulated from the information substantiating the need for change.

To make matters worse, the efficiency report mentality serves as reinforcement to the doctrine of obsolescence and renewal (see pp. 37–38). Being an annual affair applied in Vietnam to men rotating home annually, the efficiency report encourages a vision of the war blocked into neat one-year segments. It is in the nature of the efficiency report system to direct an officer's interest away from long-term projects (though he may continue to pay lip service to them). He needs — or feels he needs — to see something *new* accomplished during his twelve-month tour; that is what he gets graded on.

Where the efficiency report is the most important subjective criterion for personal advancement, the most important objective criterion is experience in "combat" and "command." Theoretically, each army rank has a command equivalent (lieutenant — platoon; captain — company, etc.) and promotion from one rank to the next is conditional in most cases on having received command experience at the equivalent level. The advantage of having combat experi-

[24] For civilian bureaucrats, read "policy" for "strategy."

ence on one's army record is obvious. The ideal position involves both combat and command, that is, command of a unit in a combat zone. This is what a career-minded officer hopes for upon arriving for a year's tour in Vietnam. But he doesn't always get it. What sometimes results can be illustrated by the case of a certain major in Vinh Long province. This major served as liaison officer between the U.S. military advisory team and the Vietnamese directors of the pacification program. It was as critical an assignment as could be had in the province. The major participated in planning, joined the Vietnamese pacification chief on inspection trips through the countryside, offered suggestions for improvement here and there. Since he was the American in closest daily contact with Vietnamese officials, his mission included keeping his countrymen informed on Vietnamese moods and preoccupations. Now one cannot gain the confidence of foreigners overnight — not anywhere and especially not in Vietnam — and it took this major some time to establish friendships and develop a feeling for the complex and subtle Vietnamese working relationships. By the fifth month the major's efforts were beginning to bear fruit — he had been invited into the homes of two or three province officials — when, abruptly, the senior U.S. military adviser in the province relieved him. He was sent to take command of a five-man subsector team operating out of a remote district town. I asked the senior adviser why. With disarming frankness he explained that he did it because he liked the major and wanted to help his career. The post as liaison officer carried no credit for "combat" or "command." As a subsector team leader in an enemy zone he would get both. Of course this meant transferring him just when he was beginning to be useful, it meant restarting the painfully slow confidence-winning process with a new liaison officer, but that couldn't be helped. No matter how outstanding his performance as liaison officer the major's career would have suffered had he stayed on. The same thing happened with a captain who acted as liaison officer to the ARVN public works division. After four months of learning the ropes and two months of effective performance, he was transferred to a subsector.[25]

Other examples, of which there are many, would only be-labor the point I am trying to make, which is this:

The military response to the Viet Cong was conditioned by a number of institutional requirements that functioned inde-pendently of and in contradiction to the military's mission in Vietnam. These requirements also encouraged cynicism in the ranks by creating a disparity between successful pursuit of the war and successful pursuit of one's military career.

---

[25] The reverse also was possible. In Vinh Long, a major heading a sub-sector team was angling to finish out his tour with some "staff" experience on the province headquarters unit.

PART FOUR

Fred

True despair is not born in the face of
stubborn adversity, or in the exhaustion of
an unequal struggle. It comes when one
ceases to understand why he is struggling
and begins to wonder whether there is any
point to it.

ALBERT CAMUS

I

HE LOOKS, I thought, like a schoolboy doing his homework; seated there, hunched over a desk, right hand bearing down on the pencil moving slowly across a sheet of paper six inches from his nose.

"Excuse me," I said.

The young man looked up, the pencil still grafted onto the paper, and he gave out a big glowing grin.

But he didn't say anything.

"May I come in?" I asked.

"Oh!" He jumped up. "Please . . . sure . . ." He was moving around the desk, still grinning, hand extended, slightly off balance. "Jesus . . . sorry . . . come on in . . . grab a seat . . ." He stood over six feet, about two hundred pounds, built like a tight end, but, as the coach would say, not mean enough. The giveaway was that grin. Blithe, boyish, all-trusting. Head cheerleader maybe, or president of his class. "My name's Fred Abramson . . . Pleased to meet you . . . Go on . . . Grab a seat . . ."

He pulled himself back onto the roof of the desk, feet dangling. He wore a pale blue oxford cloth button-down, khaki chinos, white tennis socks with red and blue stripes, loafers. He said, "Don't see many fresh American faces around here. That's a certainty."

And I, the visiting stranger, found myself injudiciously asking the question he was just coming to.

"What brings *you* to Vinh Long?"

That was early in 1967.

₩

A year and a half later — a century and a half later it seemed — I sat in the Abramsons' split-level ranch house in suburban Seattle and read the letters Fred's parents had saved since college.

"I hope to keep some of the traits, namely the generosity of the Turk and the Greek, the warmth of the Greek, the vivacity of the Italian, the flourish of the French, the honesty of the Swiss and Austrian, the *qué será* happiness of the Spanish, the interest in nature and practical things of the German and the interest in government and world affairs of the English."

He was writing from Rotterdam in the summer of 1963, twenty-one years old, about to top out a triumphal tour by taking his place in the engine room of a Norwegian freighter bound for Norfolk. Sublime, that's how he felt.

"A full man is like a tree with its roots deep in the ground, its leaves high in the sky and its fruit not only nourishing but used. Well, I'm just a sapling (and Ronnie and Craig are only saps), and have yet little fruit to bear, but I feel I've gone a little higher in the sky and a little deeper in the ground — become more idealistic and more practical, more critical and more appreciative of my country.

"My ideals for freedom, humanity, and health for all have only strengthened but I've also realized that since the apple one country has oppressed another, and one man dominated another. I think that much of this has been caused by misunderstanding and the lack of effort to understand. The first is sad, but the second is inexcusable."

And while young Frederick gloried and sweated in the engine room, the letter arrived in Seattle where it was read aloud by Doris Abramson, his mother, Harold listening gravely, the boys gulping it down in heady draughts — Ronnie and Craig, the first eighteen, the other thirteen.

Fred's successful hitchhiking tour of Europe resolved a crisis provoked a year and a half earlier when, as a college sophomore, he had it borne in upon him that all was not possible. To a young man for whom the cycle of desire, a little effort, then satisfaction, had come to be accepted as the natural order of things, the new awareness was profoundly unsettling. All the more so because Fred's goals came to him as dreams. In 1960 the dream was Europe. Stanford, his school, had a campus in France. Fred applied to spend his junior year there and was rejected.

Fred Abramson — President of the Roosevelt High School junior class, winner of the Phi Beta Kappa award, a George F. Baker scholarship, most popular student . . . rejected! Inconceivable.

But if Fred's romanticism got him into this crisis, it would also get him out. He dreamed: Who needs Stanford's French campus, anyway? It's only a crutch. The *real* way to do it is on your own. Hit the road! And, in December 1962, midway through his junior year, he did.

The legacy of Fred Abramson's voyage through Europe is

a report prepared for the George F. Baker Foundation, his benefactors, in part as a justification for absenting himself from school for a semester. A brief excerpt captures the spirit.

"In Berlin, I worked for two weeks in a refugee camp . . . One Sunday morning I took four little refugee boys to Sunday school. I dressed myself. I helped dress them and we started off. They did not know what to think of the little chapel or what was being said about God. I kept telling them to sit still, to listen to their teacher, and to behave better. Then I realized that I was not behaving myself when I was chiding them. I decided to set an example of what I believed in and hope that they might do the same. Slowly they quieted and listened. We all learned from the Sunday school lesson. On the way home we played together as we walked. It was necessary at first to show complete impartiality or one boy would feel snubbed. I loved them and they loved me. They called me 'uncle,' but I was no better than they — only larger. We influenced each other . . .

"I think often of the families I ate with and the friends I met. I hope some will be able to come to stay with me at home or at school. Now, as in later life, I want to show my people the good in 'foreigners' as well as show our neighbors the good in America . . .

"There is hope for the future. I saw it."

Fred carried his hope for the future back to Stanford and from there to Johns Hopkins Graduate School of Advanced International Studies in Washington, D.C. His letters home offered a happy mix.

October 1964: "I have a 15-minute report to give on the Nth country problem in an hour and a half. This involves the diffusion of nuclear weapons throughout the world. Now there are five nuclear powers . . ."

February 1965: "This last Friday Jim and I . . . threw a Las Vegas Party . . . In Jim's room there was a blackjack game going, in the living room socializing and roulette, and in the kitchen another roulette game. We put the vanity dresser and some other things out on the fire escape and moved my closet into the kitchen. We bought one half keg and one quarter keg of beer. We had six girls be bunnies . . . They fixed themselves up with cardboard rabbit ears and we bought some cotton to serve as bunnytails . . ."

That summer Fred went to Mexico as counselor to a group of American undergraduates participating in the Experiment in International Living program. He returned home convinced more than ever that his future lay in working with people from foreign lands. *With* them. His was a faith founded on respect — not missionary zeal, not middle class guilt.

"On the political scene, my ideals make me a socialist — not for America where . . . everybody's a capitalist — but for all the world . . . But when it comes to my sacrificing my own abundance and a few American comforts for the rest of my life it's a conservative I'll be."

‖

Harold Abramson visited Fred in the spring of 1966 while east on business. Fred told his father then that the Vietnamese people were suffering and he wanted to help them. He said he was applying for a field post with the United States Agency for International Development (USAID).

Fred received his Master's degree from Johns Hopkins in June. He arrived in Saigon the second week in July. USAID sent him to Can Tho, headquarters for IV Corps (the Delta), and from there to Vinh Long province.

"Dear folks . . .

"My job is to be a generalist . . . supervising programs from public health to education to agriculture to youth and sports to kingdom come. For the most part what I'll be doing is to try to get the Vietnamese province and district officials to do their work — to get people to walk on the sidewalks and then put a white line down the center of the road and then get people to stop at the stop signs, etc."

A few weeks later, he summed up his initial impressions in a mimeographed "Vinh Long Newsletter" to friends.

"Vietnam is the Land of Advisors. American advisors fill the streets of Saigon with noxious fumes of Ford, defoliate and depopulate I and II Corps forests with flames of war, and furnish enough aid to transform Dante's inferno into Happy Valley. In the unrelenting struggle against the VC, we use Fords, International Harvesters, and jeeps like my

own; B-52s, Beechcraft and cowlike Caribou; 105 mm. can-
nons, M-16s and mortars; bulgur wheat, cottonseed cooking
oil and medicines; communication, construction, electrification and purification. But, most of all we use paper. We
record and review; we send and receive; we count and soon
we'll be computing. But, there is a purpose for this — DECI-
SION-MAKING. Out of the paperwork jungles of Saigon, Regional headquarters and province officialdom rise mountains
and mountains of decisions. Reports are filed, decisions are
made and then piled atop one another awaiting action.
There is a logistics bottleneck here between decisionmak-
ing and relevant action. Every once in a while a decision does squeak through the pipeline (Governmentese for
'trough') . . .

"Vietnam is a land of Advisors and nationbuilding, of tall
white men running around in airconditioned circles. It's a
tight knit 300,000 persons doing their time and sharing mild
contempt and dislike for a people whose language and culture they neither know nor understand. Till I can break out
of the circle, at least to some extent, I shall continue to enjoy
an adviser's life — jolly Americans, cheap beer gardens, all
the comforts of home and better food than I've had for the
past two years."

The problem of breaking out of that circle of Americans
was eventually resolved by an act of will. Breaking into
Vietnamese circles proved more difficult. Why did they
seem so suspicious?

"It's been two months now in this town, but I still don't
feel so attached to the people. It's indescribable . . ."

Looking at them, looking at himself, trying to see them
seeing him, Fred began to feel the first pangs of doubt.

"The problem is whether actually economic development

and the western way of life is actually the best way of life. For all the comforts of home that we have, I must say that Americans are not always the happiest people in the world."

And yet:

"What the west is trying to do for the underdeveloped regions of the world is generally a good thing — to combat disease and introduce public health, to promote a broader and fuller education for more people, to make sure that they will be able to produce for themselves enough food and maybe even cash to travel, certain luxuries . . ."

All right, Fred said to himself, the objective is fair and just, and perhaps, because the challenge is so massive, a massive bureaucracy is necessary. Therefore the fault is his own. He had been too quick to reach for the cosmic image.

"Sometimes with the children so numerous and poor and poorly educated the magnitude of change necessary to come anywhere near our setup discourages even the taking of the first step in the journey of a thousand days. But, sights set from day to day can be more rewarding . . ."

By October, he had settled down.

"I work 9–10 hours a day and always 5 hours on Saturday and usually some hours on Sunday . . . Also, I study Vietnamese every night and next week I'll begin to teach a class in English two nights a week to a group of Service chiefs . . ."

As he became involved in the daily requirements, Fred found that his subordination of imagination to bureaucratic necessity was compensated by a new sense of power that, of itself and by itself, apart from results, was altogether thrilling. He had become the dispenser of all that was good; the sufferers were his supplicants. In April, with characteristic frankness, he diagnosed his new condition.

"It's amazing the kind of stuff I get to do . . . Today I signed three telegrams, two memos, told one helicopter what to do part of the day, signed off approximately 250,000 piastres ($2500) and 600 bags of cement (about $2000) and 250 pieces of rebar (about $1100) and verbally agreed to spend 250,000 piastres, about 500 bags of cement, 200 pieces of rebar and 25 large sheets of roofing ($1200) . . . I think that after I get back to the states and wherever I go and whatever I do, I'll probably miss being able to throw all the funds and personnel around that I've been doing . . ."

Fred was at a crossroads now. He had effected the intoxicating union of power with reform, the secret dream of so many liberals. He might easily have served out his tour by working to increase the scope of his power and "therefore" (Ah, sweet stuff!) of his reform, his conscience clear and his ego satisfied. But it wasn't in him. That became evident in April when the bureaucracy, pleased with his efforts, offered him a new post as director of the youth program for the entire Delta. It was a distinct promotion; moreover, coming early in his tour, it carried the possibility of an eventual plush assignment in Saigon: the summit of power and prestige and "goodworks." Fred turned it down. He explained that he wouldn't feel right leaving the province just when he was becoming effective.

Fred's personal struggle with the power instinct was not over, but he had won the first round, he had mastered the bureaucratic environment, and now he was ready to move out on his own.

But in what direction? Some months later he would write:

"I am getting over the paranoia that every one of them is trying to use me, my people and my cement, for their own purposes and ulterior motives. Maybe I'm just getting numb and less sensitive . . ."

The "they" about whom Fred wrote were not the peasants of Vinh Long. The Vietnamese Fred dealt with — the people who served as the Americans' channel of communication to the mass of the population — were civil servants. Their collective personality had been shaped by three generations of French rule, followed by independence in 1954, followed by an ever growing American "presence."

The American presence in Vietnam was notable for its ambiguity. While the reality of growing Vietnamese *dependence* on the Americans was apparent to anyone with eyes to see, the rhetoric denied it. How, then, does the dependent man demonstrate this independence so insistently demanded of him by the Americans and proclaimed to the world? He demonstrates it by treating his benefactors with contempt. Vietnamese civil servants showed their "independence" of the Americans by stealing from them. Unwittingly, the Americans had provided the Vietnamese with the incentive (undreamed of wealth) *and* the moral justification for corruption on a massive scale. Thus the Vietnamese civil servant, his conscience freed from all restraint, went out on a binge.

We Americans were like a team of doctors so preoccupied with halting a cholera epidemic in a foreign country (because it might eventually reach our shores) that we failed to notice that the people we were immunizing against cholera were already victims of endemic cirrhosis of the liver.

Meanwhile, the status of the mass of the population continued as before.

•

This, essentially, is what Fred faced in Vinh Long. He tried. He worked while they loafed, explaining that Westerners feel more at home working. He learned to look the other way while they funneled USAID construction materials, explaining, "Well, so what if it took twice as much cement to build the schoolhouse than it should have. We can afford it, and the main thing is that we have a schoolhouse."

But it seemed that each painful restructuring of his morale was met by some new incident that knocked out all the props. There was the ring of civil servants who were siphoning off construction funds — and even food — meant for the peasants. Or the members of that other clique who were having furniture made from stolen government materials, then selling it to their respective government agencies. In both cases, it turned out that the ringleaders were young middle-level civil servants, representatives of the new "French-free" generation on whom Fred had placed his hopes. In fact several of them, when they weren't stealing, attended Fred's tuition-free English class.

If only there were something to grab onto, some point where the corruption ended. He could begin there. But he couldn't find that point. Try as he might he was destined to move always in a contaminated area, himself a symbol of contamination, not a cure but an enticement.

"Since I've been over here, I've had three watches stolen — two right off my arm by little kids. They're dear little rapscallions. They crowd around and rub your arms — because Vietnamese are fascinated by body hair — and hold your hand — and slip the watch off."

III

Sometimes in the evening, while most of the advisers were watching the movie at the MACV house or writing letters home, I would drop in on Fred at his office downtown. It had become his practice to postpone much of his paperwork until after dinner so that he might use the daylight hours for field trips. Invariably, I found him hunched over a desktop that was overflowing with charts and documents. "Look at this," he would say, "I'm a goddam wastebasket." And he would laugh, and shake his head, and throw his feet up on the desk, and shake his head again and say "shit . . ." or some other expletive; and we would talk about the day's activities. He knew the province better than any American. He felt equally at ease discussing competing GVN cliques at province headquarters; the tensions between Hoa Hao and Buddhist militia units in this or that village; pending projects for construction of a footbridge in a tiny hamlet; an electrification plant in a district capital; the distribution of midwives' kits, playground equipment, machetes . . . We would talk about these things. And in the relaxed atmosphere of the evening, as Fred unwound, we would talk about the reasons why. It was only then that he let surface the doubts and competing tensions plaguing his conscience: First, he could not reconcile what he was doing with what he believed in; at the same time he was unwilling to liberate himself from responsibility by accepting what some associates called "the long view," the idea that corruption and its attendant problems are a passing byproduct of the war and

not his concern. This troubled him most. For him, the
"means" *had to* justify the end in Vietnam because our
chosen "means" was the Vietnamese government. If we won,
then the "means" would *become* the end — the government
would assume undisputed power.

Of course war breeds corruption, Fred said to me one evening. But the difference here in Vietnam, he continued, is
that the war is being fought by two factions for the loyalty of
the uncommitted masses. He shook his head.

"If only I could bring myself to believe that the faction we
are supporting cares. To me, if they don't care and we accept that, then it means we don't care ourselves what alternative the people get, just so it doesn't subscribe to *that* ideology."

Hardened revolutionaries, armor-plated with certainty,
political missionaries, satisfied that no evil is so great as the
rejection of their political faith, would find Fred Abramson a
profoundly unsympathetic figure. He could not be seduced
by power, even the power — potentially as corrupting as any
other — for doing good; he was preoccupied with "means";
he stubbornly refused to surrender his doubts *or* his hopes.

Later, he felt, there will be time for recrimination; right
now he must do all he can to make matters less bad. It is this
that made him so admirable and his situation so tragic.

He knew his job, he worked hard at it. In July 1967, just
one year after he had arrived, Fred was promoted to deputy
senior adviser in Vinh Long. At age twenty-five, he was the
youngest American to hold that rank in Vietnam.

"For myself, especially if I stay in government service, the
war has been a great career booster. Also, it has taught me
leadership, hardnosedness, just generally how to operate
from the seat of my pants."

But . . .

"So far, as I said before, results and recent developments
are not encouraging . . .   Many things I'm still learning and
others I will learn, but the leadership, advisory, and memo-
writing experience gained by Fred Abramson is not justification for such a monumental misspent effort."

That was the other thing.
On the one hand, corruption; on the other, misdirection
and inefficiency and ambition.

"The huge American effort here makes me sad because it's
so inefficient and sometimes I think even wrongheaded . . .
Why is this affluent air-conditioned war so goddamned inefficient?

"Partly because so many goodhearted people are mis-
guided and commitments must be honored — in terms of national pride, political theories, in terms of bureaucratic and
business interests. When I first came over here I had my res-
ervations about this war but I used to ask myself what would
I do if I were President Johnson and I would think that
maybe he is right to continue the cause as he was going. But
not now. Not now . . ."

By then (October), security was beginning to deteriorate
in the province. The Viet Cong had initiated the squeeze
that would reach its climax four months later, during Tet.
Fred reacted by working even harder. His family did not
hear from him at all in November. They worried and wrote
and, at last . . .

"A lot of water over the bridge. Or so it seems. And the
PX was closed today. And I learned the number of outposts
in Chau Thanh district today. And I can never hope to un-

derstand this war and how can the U.S. public ever understand this thing over here . . .

"A big explosion just went off but it wasn't big enough. I think it was one of those skygoing firecrackers that we shot off in Lake Forest Park that night. Reminisce. You know, and you just know what it is like to think of the old days. And remember moments . . . I can remember going over to David and George Scott's house and Ronnie chewing Susan Evans' bubble gum and swiping . . ."

And that was all.

IV

During November the number of Viet Cong incidents in Vinh Long had jumped to 153, more than double the monthly average. The record rate continued into December. District towns were mortared, government patrols ambushed, outposts overrun. Persons driving down normally secure roads came under fire. It got so bad that two district chiefs refused to leave their towns unless supported by a full-scale military operation. The enemy seemed to be lurking everywhere. At this point, the senior adviser departed for a thirty-day skiing holiday in California.

He wasn't bugging out. His leave time had been requested and approved months before.

The senior adviser departed on December 15, the chain of command clanked forward, and Fred Abramson, now an aging twenty-six, felt himself being lifted, helplessly . . .

"Today, I became king for a month and a week. Col. Roberge, an intelligent, effective and fine leader of men, departed for the States, as they're called, on home leave . . . Can you imagine me being the adviser to a Vietnam Province Chief and the commander, if temporary, of a team of 40 officers, 60–70 enlisted men, and 20 civilians, not counting the MILPHAP and Seabee teams?

"Well, time to be on to bed . . .

"I miss you all very, very much."

A few days later the new acting senior adviser went on his first military operation. He returned late that afternoon.

"How did it go?" asked Lieutenant Colonel Jenne, the number three man in the Vinh Long advisory hierarchy, now acting deputy to Fred.

"Oh all right, I guess," Fred said.

"Little muddy there."

"Yeah," Fred said, grinning his grin. "I didn't feel I should pretend to be a soldier, but I think you'd better have the supply officer get me some fatigues. I felt kind of conspicuous out there."

He had gone on the operation wearing khaki chinos and a polo shirt.

Fred went on military operations regularly after that, wearing his new fatigues and combat boots. He could never bring himself to carry a weapon.

For some, the military side of the war, though more dangerous, has one great advantage over the civilian side. It is clear-cut. There is you, and there is the enemy. From Fred's perspective, however, it was impossible to separate the impact of a military operation on the enemy from its impact on the people. Now, as director of military as well as civilian operations, he became prisoner to a new kind of tension. It crept out late in December at the daily briefing. The operations officer (S-3), a major, was recapping a successful district operation the day before: "One B-40 rocket launcher captured, four VC k-i-a, two PF k-i-a, one civilian w-i-a . . ." Fred interrupted him. Civilian? What kind of civilian? How did a civilian get involved in an operation? The S-3 didn't know. He only had the statistics. It would be a good idea to find out, the acting senior adviser said. If the civilian was an innocent victim there should be some compensation. He cited a directive on compensation. Find out who the civilian was, Fred ordered. The S-3 nodded. He was about to continue when an officer in the back said,

"I spoke with one of the advisers in the operation. It was a fourteen-year-old girl. She got caught in a crossfire. She was wounded, and this afternoon she died."

Fred asked the S-3 to find out how that happened. Then he turned and searched the audience with his eyes until he found the civilian responsible for refugees.

"You had better see about compensation," Fred said. He faced front.

The major, visibly uncomfortable, was about to recommence when Fred turned around again.

"And find out what you can about the family," he said.

Now he faced front again. "All right," he said, "you can continue now."

V

On January 6, Fred was driving up Route 7A, he was just three miles from the province capital, when he was blown out of his jeep by a B-40 rocket fired at point-blank range. Dazed, bleeding, he scrambled along the muddy roadbed. An automatic rifle bullet tore into his chest and he fell on his face in the mud and died, about thirty feet from the smoking jeep.

POSTSCRIPT

Subject: Death of Fred Abramson
Action Taken: See Below

The government responded to Fred Abramson's death with
efficiency. Mr. and Mrs. Abramson were telephoned within
hours by Shirley Weinstein, a State Department official in
Washington. At the parents' request, Miss Weinstein got
hold of the United States Embassy in Ghana. An embassy
official immediately contacted Fred's brother, Ron, twenty-
two, a Peace Corps English teacher. Ron was flown home via
London at U.S. government expense, arriving January 9.
The body, scrubbed clean, arrived a day later. USAID sent
a representative to the funeral on January 12, the same day
that General Westmoreland signed a letter of condolence. A
similar letter crossed President Johnson's desk on January 17.
The only snag, a minor one, had to do with Fred's personal
effects, which were misrouted. They did not reach Seattle
until the following October.

PART FIVE

Forward into the Past

VINH LONG — half in ruin when I left in March — was by December a changed city. Or so it appeared. Much of the destruction had been repaired. The once deserted streets were again filled with people, and the air at the U.S. advisory team headquarters was filled with statistics suggesting — *progress.* "On every front." The optimism seemed so intense, the activity so frenetic that the initial impact was dizzying.

According to the best intelligence estimates, Viet Cong provincial and main force battalions were operating at half strength. No major engagement had been initiated by a Viet Cong battalion since August. Meanwhile, Viet Cong were surrendering in droves — nearly one thousand had turned themselves in during the past five months in Vinh Long alone.

Conclusion: The Viet Cong had been badly mauled during Tet, but, due to panic and confusion on our side, the enemy had gained a "psychological victory." Finally, in August, after one last desperate offensive, the bubble burst. The Viet Cong effort collapsed.

Our response? Look around:

PF. Popular Forces militia who staff the outposts scattered over the countryside. Top priority now. Increased in strength by 20 percent and armed with the deadly U.S. M-16 automatic rifle.

APC. Accelerated Pacification Campaign. Launched in November to "radically increase the speed of GVN expansion in the countryside." [1] Vinh Long's "budget": fifty-six hamlets, each marked for a government cadre team plus 100,000 piastres' worth of improvements.

AIK. A long-standing revolving cash fund bankrolled by the United States now being exploited effectively for the first time. Purpose: To provide financing for "high impact" projects that might otherwise become bottled up in the GVN bureaucracy — schools in newly "liberated" areas, saturation propaganda campaigns, intelligence programs . . . Monthly AIK outlays were up from 600,000 piastres in July to 6,000,-000 piastres in November.

MAT. Five-man U.S. Army Mobile Advisory Teams who live with the PF militia, train them in the use of the M-16, in night patrolling and ambushes. Vinh Long had twelve MAT units. Eighteen more had been requested.

It was ironic. Now, just as we were making noises about an American pullout from Vietnam, we were closer to victory than ever before. Just a little longer . . .

I listened to all this, in conversations and in briefings, and I moved through the countryside, which seemed to have taken on some of the aspects of a workshop — *so* much construction, *so* much activity — and, well, goddammit, maybe we *had* pulled it off.

◢

[1] From a U.S. Government memorandum.

The return to reality began as I went over the basic figures on population control — how many people belonged to "us" and how many to "them." It was difficult to make precise comparisons because methods of collecting data had changed. When I first came to Vietnam, in January 1967, the standard method was to rate hamlets as "GVN," "Contested," or "VC." (See Appendix A.) That month, however, the Americans (but not GVN), began experimenting with a complex Hamlet Evaluation System (HES). Each American district adviser was required to take what amounted to a monthly multiple choice exam for each hamlet in his district. Sample questions:

> Did a significant number of families move to the immediate vicinity of this hamlet during the past month?
>
> 0. No
> 1. Yes, primarily from insecure areas
> 2. Yes, but not primarily from insecure areas
> 3. Unknown
>
> Did armed enemy military forces enter this hamlet during the month?
>
> 0. No
> 1. Yes, but only once
> 2. Yes, 2 to 4 times
> 3. Yes, more than 4 times
>
> Have there been any enemy-organized public meetings or group activities (demonstrations, propagandizing, drafting porters and laborers, recruiting, etc.) in or near this hamlet during the month?
>
> 0. No
> 1. Yes, but only once
> 2. Yes, more than once[2]

[2] I first learned about this Hamlet Evaluation System during a visit to a district in Vinh Long in 1967. "Well, end of the month . . . time to fill out these fucking idiot sheets," the district adviser had said.

Next, each hamlet was awarded an over-all rating: A, B, C, D, E, or V. Hamlets rated A, B, or C were recorded as "GVN," D and E as "Contested"; V hamlets belonged to the Viet Cong.

During November and December 1967, the tempo of enemy activity in the countryside reached ominous proportions. Frightened district chiefs were refusing to leave their district towns, roads were being closed to government traffic. But the HES figures did not budge. November: 58 percent GVN control. December: 58 percent.

In January 1968, the acting senior adviser and five other Americans were killed in an ambush on a "secure" road. Viet Cong began to move into many other heretofore tranquil areas, according to our own intelligence. Still the HES figures held firm! January: 58 percent GVN control. Then the roof fell in. (See pp. 120–134.)

Thus, during those critical months, when we were losing ground everywhere but on the briefing charts, the Hamlet Evaluation System did not respond to reality.

In February 1968, after the Tet attacks, GVN-controlled population plummeted to 35 percent on the HES charts. Taken at face value — which is the way evaluators in Saigon and Washington take them when it is in their interest — we suffered a tremendous defeat during Tet: Almost half the population previously under our control had been lost overnight.

But let's be fair. Government forces had retreated into defensive positions around the cities and the advisers filling out the HES sheets for February simply assumed that most of the countryside belonged to the Viet Cong. The same held true for March. Then in April government troops began to

---

This district adviser and others explained to me that HES demanded an intimate knowledge of hamlet life after dark that in many cases could not be obtained unless they were actually living in the hamlet.

probe outward and the charts began to probe upward. April: 41 percent GVN control. May: 44 percent. June: 52 percent.

The revision was based primarily on the *resistance* the advancing troops met. We were going after territory occupied by the Viet Cong during Tet, we were meeting minimal resistance, we were reoccupying the territory. But had it been occupied by the Viet Cong during Tet? We think so. We assume so. More to the point: What does "occupy" mean? To us? To the Viet Cong?

In the fall of 1968, the hamlet control percentage figures crept up and up past the pre-Tet figures and American evaluators reported a new dimension had been breached. The increases were a percentage point per month until November when they spurted by four percentage points, i.e., 20,000 Vinh Long inhabitants living in contested or outright Viet Cong areas came under government control in November 1968.

November was also the first month of APC — the Accelerated Pacification Campaign.

APC

In October 1968 a secret memorandum went out to province senior advisers from the U.S. Command in Saigon. The memo reported high-level American concern that the Viet Cong might demand a cease-fire, then try to enter negotiations as the rightful representatives of the population under their control. In the Delta this would put them on a parity with GVN, even by our own statistical reckoning. "To preempt this possibility, drastic action . . . is believed necessary," the memo stated. Our counter-strategy, as unfolded in the memo, was to establish a minimum of GVN "presence" over as wide an area as possible, thereby cutting down the territory over which the Viet Cong could lay undisputed claim. Hence the Accelerated Pacification Campaign. As an essentially political strategy, APC made sense. The trouble was that it didn't remain a political strategy.

The Accelerated Pacification Campaign began on November 1. On that date the 1968 pacification program was prematurely halted. Pacification teams were withdrawn from their respective hamlets (twenty-two hamlets in Vinh Long) without regard to their rate of progress in those hamlets. The teams were transferred to newly designated APC hamlets.

Vinh Long was assigned forty APC hamlets. Since there weren't enough cadre teams to go around, the three-month APC program was divided into two six-week phases. During the first six weeks — November 1 to December 14 — cadre teams would pacify twenty-two hamlets. During the second phase — December 14 to February 1 — they would pacify eighteen more.

On December 6, all province senior advisers in the Delta were summoned to a meeting at IV Corps headquarters in Can Tho. APC is going better than expected, the senior advisers were told; how many *more* hamlets can you absorb into the program? Vinh Long opted for twelve more hamlets, bringing their three-month obligation to fifty-six — one-fifth the hamlets in the province.

The cadre who were rushed in and out of these fifty-six hamlets between November and the end of January were told to satisfy four criteria:

1. Identify the Viet Cong infrastructure.
2. Organize a people's self-defense force.
3. Organize a hamlet election.
4. Initiate at least two self-help projects.

To accomplish that much in forty days was of course impossible; it was strictly a propaganda exercise. "The name of the game," an American pacification adviser told me, "is planting the government flag."

But it didn't stop there. As the symbolic flag was planted in an APC hamlet that hamlet was upgraded on the Hamlet Evaluation System charts. The result was that symbolic acts were converted into hard statistical realities. That sudden quantum jump in government-controlled population in November, as "authenticated" by HES, was attributable to the Accelerated Pacification Campaign.

The HES figures did not reflect reality on the ground. But they did reflect *a kind of* reality that, in a strange way, was more believable than what was actually happening. It was more believable because Americans could work with it — accept it, refute it, modify it. The HES figures (and similar devices) carried us into a new matrix more congenial to our senses.

Within the new matrix a debate was carried out. The debate centered on the extent of "progress" against the Viet Cong.

On one side in the debate were the true believers. These people — in Vinh Long, in Saigon, in Washington — many of them already concerned that the administration was planning a sellout, grabbed at the hollow statistics, proclaiming,

"Look! The Viet Cong are crumbling! Victory is in sight! Just a little longer . . ."

Others took a more sophisticated position. They said,

"We *seem* to be making progress. We are moving into new areas. The Viet Cong are not responding.

"On the other hand, we had *seemed* to be making progress prior to the Tet Offensive . . .

"Now, personally, we feel today's progress is more real.

"The Viet Cong are weaker. Here, look at these statistics on VC strength.

"The government is stronger. Here, look at these statistics on the GVN military buildup . . .

"On the other hand, it would be naïve to say victory is just around the corner.

"But we're on the right track. For example, look at these Accelerated Pacification Campaign statistics . . .

"Of course, we all know that GVN is merely establishing a 'presence' in these hamlets. No one would say they are one hundred percent secure . . .

"But let's face it. Nothing is one hundred percent secure in South Vietnam . . ."

Back and forth, back and forth. Newspapers picked up the beat.

On January 31, 1969, the *New York Times* carried a report on the Accelerated Pacification Campaign from a respected veteran correspondent.

The correspondent judiciously presented the pros and cons. He pointed out that most newly pacified hamlets were ranked C on the Hamlet Evaluation System scale, which meant they just barely qualified for "secure" status.

"It is conceded," the correspondent wrote, "that such a hamlet could be *overrun* by a large Vietcong force, but it is regarded as essentially in government control." (Italics added.)

Elsewhere in the same article the correspondent remarked that "the Vietcong is expected to *attack* many of the newly pacified hamlets — but no concerted enemy effort has yet been made." (Italics added.)

Attack! Overrun! This is language we all understand. But do the Viet Cong understand it? During 1967, more than twenty hamlets were pacified in Vinh Long province. Yet, as we know from the cases of Ap Bay, Ap Tan Qui and others, the hamlets were pacified in name only. The Viet Cong did not have to win these hamlets back — they did not have to *overrun* them, they did not have to *attack* them — because they had never really lost them, *except on our progress charts.*

The major believed it.

"You'll really be surprised," he said, as our sampan with its little outboard motor chugged away from the dock at Vinh Long city. The major was the American adviser for Chau Thanh district which consists of the province capital and its environs.

Our sampan moved up the canal out of the city proper and the jungle closed in. The major was cheerful. He explained how only a few weeks ago this stretch or that stretch was infested with Viet Cong and passage would have been impossible.

"Now we have them on the run," he said.

We stopped at an outpost recently occupied by a platoon of Popular Forces militia and a U.S. Mobile Advisory Team (MAT). The Americans — an army captain, a lieutenant, three sergeants — were helping the PF construct housing for their dependents.

Further upstream, another MAT unit was helping a PF platoon construct a new outpost that would be occupied by still another PF platoon.

"We're really moving out," the major said.

After the trip, we had lunch with some Catholic priests at a seminary on the outskirts of Vinh Long city. (Vietnamese dishes, Algerian wine, French brandy, Scotch whisky, conversation in English.)

"Well, what do you think now?" the major said. "How does it compare with last March?"

I agreed that there was no comparison — things looked much better now — but I could not follow him to his conclusion that the Viet Cong were collapsing. I could not because my memory moved back beyond March and February into 1967, when the major, who did not arrive in Vinh Long until the late summer of 1968, was stationed in Pennsylvania. I remembered trips through these same canals in Chau Thanh in 1967. There was no problem. Chau Thanh district was secure. In fact, during the first seven months of 1967, *not a single Viet Cong incident* was recorded in Chau Thanh district. It was not until August 1967, when they were preparing their big offensive, that the Viet Cong moved into Chau Thanh in force, primarily to clear the way for the invasion of the province capital. Now, evidently, daytime security was being restored.

Nighttime security remained marginal. Over the past four months, a monthly average of eighteen Viet Cong incidents had been recorded in Chau Thanh district. The incident level is not an absolute indicator, but it does help show that, comparatively speaking, Chau Thanh was better than it was in February 1968, but worse than it was in 1967.

Later that same day, I checked the Vinh Long advisory team personnel records. Only one soldier — a sergeant who had extended his tour — had been stationed in Vinh Long as recently as 1967. To me, Vinh Long seemed to be returning to its 1967 level when we were still a long way from victory. To the Vinh Long advisory team, who had only the Tet catastrophe as a basis for comparison, the Viet Cong were crumbling.

This isolation from the past is only half — the lesser half — of a bizarre condition that affects the understanding of Americans in Vietnam as to what is happening around them.

There is also a particular isolation from the future. It comes across strongest in the MAT program.

MAT

In Saigon, I had read reports documenting the impact of the new Mobile Advisory Team program. Here a MAT-reinforced PF platoon had held out against a Viet Cong battalion; there a PF platoon had ambushed a Viet Cong company. I reserved judgment, though, because in Saigon, where one can draw on reports of thousands of individual actions nationwide, it is possible to collect spot evidence that can be used to dramatize the "success" of almost any program.

But (and here is the key) any judgment, if it is to be meaningful, must go beyond the measure of immediate impact. In Vietnam, American *novelty* plus American *priority resources* equals immediate impact every time.

An American Mobile Advisory Team is a companion element to a Vietnamese PF platoon for three months. After that the team moves on to another PF platoon. Most of the accounts of PF successes came out of this three-month period — when the PF were receiving special attention, when they were trying out an exciting new weapon (the M-16), when a highly skilled American unit was fighting alongside them, when due to the presence of this American unit they could be assured of priority ground, air, and artillery support; when, in short, they were receiving a jolt that might be compared to an injection of Dexedrine.

One night I heard a MAT leader proudly describe how he had scrounged a mortar for "my" PF platoon, and how the mortar had given the platoon new confidence. "Where are you getting ammunition for the mortar?" I asked. He

winked. "I'm scrounging that too." The American was showing laudable American ingenuity. He had developed his own
supply channel. It did not occur to him that the supply
channel would dry up when he left.

It was the same old problem. The MAT leader was graded
by his superiors on his performance during a three-month
period. The only measurement of his performance: the performance of "his" PF platoon. Consequently, he did everything he could to get that platoon *moving right now*. Army
public information officers recorded his successes for the
folks back home. News correspondents visited him in the
field. Then the Mobile Advisory Team left and the public
information officers and the correspondents moved on to
other newly installed MAT units. More successes. It was
just like Ap Tan Qui and Ap Tan Thang.[3] (See pp. 31–33.)

AIK

The deployment of the APC cadre teams and the MAT advisory units was accompanied by a great deal of American-
financed construction — schools, offices, warehouses — in
the district towns and the villages and the hamlets. Many of
the Americans in Vinh Long talked excitedly about the salu-
tary impact of this construction on the people's "morale" —
an uncomfortably familiar word. The reasoning, also familiar, was that we would rebuild what the Viet Cong destroyed,
thereby causing the enemy to suffer by comparison.

The weakness of the construction syndrome is that the
people, as has been demonstrated time and again, look upon

[3] The Accelerated Pacification Campaign showed elements of this same
problem. No one looked back. So long as the cadre teams kept moving
success would seem continuous. (1966 revisited. See pp. 15–16.)

these gifts with indifference. Under AIK, this weakness was compounded: In the past, at least construction had been programmed through GVN channels; now it was coming for the most part directly from the Americans' AIK fund. Now the people *and* the government were short-circuited. It was simply an American dole.

Meanwhile, GVN officials, whom theoretically we were helping to help themselves, found it much easier and cheaper just to let the Americans do it. It is hard to say exactly how this affected *their* morale, but one can be sure that it did nothing to stir their sense of initiative.[4]

While going over the AIK ledgers, I remarked with some surprise that the Americans were funding the construction of outposts.

For a long time, offensive-minded American officers had been trying without success to wrench GVN away from its dependence on static outpost defense. Then came Tet. While Vinh Long city was still smoking, a senior American military officer told me that the one good thing to come out of the Tet Offensive was the destruction or abandonment of eighty of the 290 outposts in the province. This is why it came as such a surprise to learn that now, in Vinh Long in December 1968, eleven months after Tet, a major outpost construction effort was under way, *financed with American funds.*

---

[4] Initiative was stirred in other quarters, however. The Vinh Long AIK ledgers for December show 105,000 piastres for a Catholic school and 217,375 piastres for a Hoa Hao refugee center. Coals to Newcastle. No two groups in the Delta are more strongly anti-Viet Cong than the Catholics and Hoa Hao (a politico-religious sect). For a "high impact" program aimed at winning people *away* from the Viet Cong, to finance projects for Catholics and Hoa Hao just doesn't make sense. As best as I could determine, these projects came on the heels of initiatives by Catholics and Hoa Hao, who cultivate the Americans and know a good thing when they see one.

The rationale was that people in a hamlet felt more "se-cure" with an outpost nearby, that an outpost meant that GVN had returned to "stay," that these were not really out-posts but "operating bases" for PF forays against the Viet Cong. Perhaps more significantly, outpost construction re-sulted in a number of positive statistical indicators that GVN was "extending" its "control." I have bracketed all these words with quotation marks because they all are illusory. If outposts made a difference the war would have been won twenty years ago. Outposts were symptomatic of a mentality that sacrificed victory (partly because to go after victory raised the specter of possible defeat) for a static equilibrium. No amount of rationalizing could change this. The presence of the MAT units in certain outposts had generated an initial élan to the construction program. The élan would last as long as the MAT units remained, perhaps a little longer. Then the old 1967 equilibrium would return.

"*No!*" said the American advisers. It will not return. The Viet Cong are not responding, they are weaker in numbers, they are confronting a defection rate of astonishing propor-tions.

Let's look at the collapsing Viet Cong.

Americans in Vinh Long attached great significance to the fact that no battalion-size attack had been launched by the Viet Cong since August. By 1968 standards, that was pretty good. But, again, 1967 was something else. During *all* of 1967, only one battalion-size attack was initiated by the Viet Cong.

Similarly, intelligence briefers in December 1968 empha-sized their arguments about a Viet Cong collapse by citing low strength figures for Viet Cong battalions operating in Vinh Long: 306th Battalion, 200 men; 308th, 200 men; 312th, 200 men; D857a, 125 men; D857b, 150 men; 509th,

150 men. The strength figures certainly were low. The trouble was that this analysis included one battalion that had been created specifically for the Tet Offensive (308th) and two battalions that had been formed since the Tet Offensive. Though the number of men per Viet Cong battalion had dropped, the number of battalions had *doubled* since mid-1967.

Below the battalions in the enemy's order of battle are the DCUs — District Concentrated Units. In April 1967, before the Viet Cong began their Tet buildup, each district in Vinh Long had one DCU, making for a combined strength estimated at 500 men. In December 1968, when the Viet Cong were "collapsing," the DCU combined strength was reported by our intelligence briefers as *down* to 665 men. Down? Of course. Down from the Tet peaks. But by a year-to-year standard, it was up. In fact, Tam Binh and Vung Liem districts now had two DCUs each, compared to one each in 1967.[5]

There remained the matter of the Viet Cong defectors. They were coming in at a remarkable rate. The rush started in August with 103 defectors, double the previous month and well above any monthly figure in 1967. By November that record figure had more than doubled again to 238, and in December it reached 303, as compared to 35 in December 1967, i.e., nearly ten times as many Viet Cong defected in December 1968 as had in December 1967. *That* was something.

The August jump in the defection rate coincided with the movement of ARVN and RF/PF troops into areas of the

[5] I enter into this numbers game *not* to prove that any Viet Cong are weak or strong. I don't know. The point is that any correspondence with reality of optimistic conclusions drawn from these statistics must be judged coincidental.

province that, reportedly, had been "liberated" by the Viet Cong. To their surprise, the advancing troops encountered little resistance, but many defectors. These events coincided also with the arrival in Vinh Long of a new senior adviser, Lieutenant Colonel Paul E. Suplizio.

Suplizio carried impressive credentials. A 1953 graduate of West Point, he also had studied at Harvard, obtaining a Master's degree in public administration and passing his oral examinations for a doctorate in political science. From Harvard he went to West Point as an assistant professor of economics, to the operations staff in Saigon (directly under General Westmoreland), to the Command and General Staff College at Fort Leavenworth, Kansas, where he wrote "A Study of the Military Support of Pacification in South Vietnam: April 1964–April 1965," [6] then to the Pentagon, and, in 1967, back to Saigon, this time as a member of the famous "Komer group" overseeing the pacification effort. Suplizio had as rich a background in counterinsurgency theory as any American in South Vietnam. He recognized the subtleties of guerrilla warfare, he opposed heavy commitments of American troops and airpower, he favored a sophisticated application of pacification techniques. He was enlightened, articulate, a pleasure to talk to. This is what makes his response to the Viet Cong especially interesting.

On September 3, Suplizio unveiled what was to become recognized as a remarkably innovative contribution to the war effort: the "third party inducement" program. Cash rewards were offered to persons who induced Viet Cong to defect.

The response was tremendous. It was so tremendous that it attracted the attention of the planners in Saigon.

[6] The book-length document was immediately stamped secret by the Army. When the national interest permits declassification, Suplizio plans to submit his report to Harvard as his doctoral dissertation.

In November, Suplizio's scheme was instituted nation-wide.[7]

Within a short time, the U.S. Mission had begun celebrating new successes in the struggle against the Viet Cong. During the week of November 17–23, according to one press release, 644 defectors were reported nationwide, the highest weekly figure since the week of April 8–15, 1967. The announcement concluded:

"The high returnee rate last week is largely a result of the successful initiation of the third party awards system throughout the country."

Back to Vinh Long.

I started with the defector tally sheets. These list the name, age, rank, home district, and length of service of each returning Viet Cong. What stood out first, even on casual reading, was the length of service. Overwhelmingly, the returnees had been Viet Cong for less than eleven months. In August, 90 percent of the defectors had served eleven months or less; September, 83 percent; October, 93 percent; November, 91 percent; December, 92 percent. Of those who had served twelve months or more, about half came from outside Vinh Long.[8] For the flood tide months of November and December, out of 541 Viet Cong ralliers, 46 had served one year or more, and of these 46, there were 26 who came from Vinh Long province. Thus, fewer than 5 percent of the defectors had served a year or more with the Viet Cong.

[7] The third party inducement program was grafted onto the already functioning "Open Arms" program created to handle Viet Cong defectors.

The memorandum circulated among senior advisers in the Delta announcing the new third party scheme stated:

"It should be noted that the whole project is patterned after the special rewards program for the payment of third parties initiated by Vinh Long on 3 September 1968."

[8] This is not surprising. A defecting Viet Cong is safer from reprisal when he surrenders at a location distant from his home unit.

When you subtract Viet Cong whose service was exactly one year, which means they were probably recruited for the Tet Offensive, the figure drops to eight.

In sum, eight defectors out of the 541 who surrendered in Vinh Long in November and December had served more than a year with the Viet Cong in Vinh Long. The so-called "Open Arms" program had scarcely touched the Viet Cong hard core. The Viet Cong who were collapsing were fresh recruits.

All right. But why so many fresh recruits? The Viet Cong have been recruiting for years without any such spilloff. The explanation comes in three parts, listed below in ascending order of importance.

First: The nature of Viet Cong recruitment changed drastically after Tet. After Tet, GVN in Vinh Long abandoned most of the countryside. The Viet Cong were able to move freely across wide areas. Obviously, many persons who at this time were brought under Viet Cong "control" and were assigned membership in Viet Cong associations were accepting their fate passively. As they had in this manner "collapsed" to the Viet Cong, so they might just as well "collapse" right back to GVN.

Second: It appears that during July, Viet Cong began confiscating the peasants' government identity cards.[9] A man without an identity card is considered ipso facto a Viet Cong suspect. In August, government troops moved into areas where the cards had been confiscated. The cardless peasants were faced with two options:

(a) They could "defect" under the GVN "Open Arms" program. In this case, they would get two new sets of clothes worth 1000 piastres, a thirty-piastre daily allowance for food, and a welcome package containing soap, chewing

[9] Reports of identity card confiscations appear repeatedly in the intelligence file kept by the Americans in Vinh Long.

gum, and other goodies; after a forty-five-day period of indoctrination at the comfortable Vinh Long "Open Arms" center, they would be handed 200 piastres in pocket money and set free.

(b) They could sit tight and risk capture and imprisonment, or worse.

Which option would *you* exercise?

Third: The celebrated third party inducement program was an open invitation to corruption.

I first became suspicious of the program while sitting in at the daily briefing in the lounge at the advisory team headquarters. The "Open Arms" adviser stepped forward to give his report:

"Sir, I have the statistics for this week. We received sixty-two returnees. And I am happy to say, sir, that every one of them came in through your third party inducement plan."

After the briefing, I walked over to the "Open Arms" adviser.

"Did you say that *every* returnee last week had an inducer?"

"That's right. The program is really going fine."

"Have you an extra copy of the rewards scale?"

The rewards were scaled according to rank, from 250,000 piastres for the chief Viet Cong commissar in the Delta to 1000 piastres for a member of a hamlet farmer's association. Most of the returnees were identified on the tally sheets as hamlet guerrillas. The reward for a hamlet guerrilla: 3000 piastres. To a peasant, living at close to a subsistence level, the reward is astronomical. Would a bogus inducer–Viet Cong arrangement involve any risk? So far as I could ascertain, very little. It was enough for the returnee to say, "I was a Viet Cong," for the reward to be paid to his "inducer." And nothing would happen to the returnee either, except that he would receive a gift package, a thirty-piastre daily allowance

for forty-five days, two new sets of clothes, and a parting gift
of 200 piastres.

I sought out someone who had interrogated returnees.

"It's amazing how little most of them know," the interroga-
tor said. "I talked to a squad leader yesterday who couldn't
remember anything he had done for the Viet Cong."

"How long had he been a Viet Cong?"

"He told me a year." (One of the elite returnees.)

"How old was he?"

"Fourteen."

"Who was his inducer?"

"I'm not absolutely sure. I think it was a relative."

The reward paid to a relative (perhaps a friend) for "in-
ducing" this fourteen-year-old "squad leader" suffering from
amnesia was 7000 piastres.

"How is this money paid out?" I asked the American in
charge of the AIK fund.

"It goes through the Open Arms center. They pass it on to
the district chief who passes it on to the inducer."

"Do Americans witness the money being paid to the inducer?"

"How can we? We just give it to the Open Arms people
and assume it gets there . . . Why do you ask?"

What clinched it was the report on the late December
graduating class from the Open Arms center. Of this class of
145 "defectors," 142 elected to return to their home hamlets.

If he had indeed left the Viet Cong the last place a defector would return to is his home hamlet. He would live in constant fear of Viet Cong reprisal.

✍

So the Americans plunged ahead, overjoyed at the collapse of the Viet Cong, determined to make the collapse even more complete by making freedom even more "attractive." During the last week in December, the American engineer adviser unveiled plans for a new Open Arms center, to be built (of course) with American AIK funds: 2,400,000 piastres. The new center would feature individual bunks, a greater luxury than could be had even at the Vinh Long municipal hospital.

Sitting at the MACV bar one hot afternoon, drinking a beer and going over my notes on the Open Arms program, I had a fantasy.

I was moving along a jungle trail under a hot Delta sun. Suddenly the damp earth under my feet turned to asphalt. Then the jungle gave way and now I was walking up an asphalt path winding through a manicured garden toward a portico that shaded the entrance to (my God!) a pink Hilton-esque concrete structure rising sixteen balconied stories into the clear blue sky. Off to the right, behind a hedge of boug-ainvillaea, the top tier of a diving board was visible. I was pouring water from my canteen onto a handkerchief when two Vietnamese peasants shuffled past. A doorman dressed in violet with gold buttons appeared and said,

"Papers, please . . ."

Soiled papers changed hands.

"Ah, yes. Excellent! Your check will be forwarded in the mail."

One of the peasants turned and headed back toward the jungle. To the other, the doorman said,

"And you, sir. Welcome!"

The Viet Cong in Vinh Long may have been collapsing.

But if this was the case, the Americans in Vinh Long did not know about it. They could not know about it. They were living in a dream world. It was an active dream world. A great deal was happening. To them, it had all become quite real. That was the chilling feature. Only one American that I talked to in Vinh Long showed the least doubt about the validity of the Open Arms program, the MAT units, the outpost construction fiesta . . . It had nothing to do with intelligence or direct perception. It was simply that the grounds for suspicion existed in another world.

Unfortunately, that other world was the world of Vietnam.

The Mang Thit Canal Again

On August 16, 1968, one year and six months after the Mang Thit project was launched and exactly a year after Premier Ky presided at those explosive ceremonies declaring the canal "open," Lieutenant Colonel Suplizio wrote pacification director Komer that "your" canal is now open. Three recent operations along the canal had put the "finishing touches" on the remaining battered Viet Cong, Suplizio wrote.

Five days later, a Vietnamese River Assault Group moving down the canal was ambushed three times in broad daylight. Eight men were killed and fifty-four wounded. The Viet Cong ambushers took no known losses.

When I arrived in December the "open" canal was off limits to Vietnamese Navy patrols, as it had been since the August ambush. I revisited Minh Duc on the north and Tra On on the south and spent Christmas Eve in Tam Binh which borders the canal halfway up. Nothing had changed.

There was a Christmas Eve party organized by the Tam Binh American advisory team. Among those attending was a young captain assigned to a nearby MAT unit. An idealistic guy. Late that night we walked into town and sipped tea at a café. It was awfully hot. My shirt clung wherever it touched. He told me, "Now my PF platoon is really respond-ing"; and he kept insisting that "you must have faith." I liked him. He reminded me of Fred. A few weeks later his PF platoon was ambushed. The young captain was killed. The two other Americans on that mission were killed also. By coincidence, all the PF survived.

APPENDICES

Appendix A

The Government

The ranking government official in Vinh Long is the Province Chief, an ARVN colonel.[1] Directly under him are a Deputy Province Chief for Security, an ARVN lieutenant colonel, and a Deputy Province Chief for Administration, a civilian. The latter two men direct the separate military and civilian bureaucracies in the province. The military organization follows the standard form — operations staff, intelligence staff, etc. The civil administration exercises responsibility over two broad areas. The first groups such static services as telecommunications and tax collection. The second area, which concerns this study, has a name: New Life Development (NLD). To borrow from an official description, NLD is "the general term applied to programs designed to bring about the development of a new society in Vietnam."

Here in outline form are the principal NLD divisions in Vinh Long:

[1] At this writing all Province Chiefs in South Vietnam are ARVN officers.

A. NLD Services in Support of Pacification

1. Public Works — roads, bridges, ferries, water supply
2. Agricultural Service — farm production, rice production, crop protection, agricultural extension
3. Agricultural Development Bank — loans to farmers
4. Fisheries
5. Cooperatives
6. Animal Husbandry
7. Land Reform
8. Social Welfare
9. Youth and Sports
10. Normal College
11. Polytechnical School
12. Provincial Health
13. Relief Commodities

B. NLD Programs Directly Involved in Pacification

"These programs are designed to bring about an immediate change in the status of life in rural areas and attempt to satisfy long-standing needs and aspirations of hamlet residents." [2]

1. Warehousing — storage of pacification materials
2. Transportation — bringing materials to rural areas
3. Rural Education
4. Rural Health
5. Public Works
6. Public Administration — mainly training hamlet and village officials
7. Agriculture and Related Activities

[2] From a U.S. Government brochure. As is apparent, some of these divisions are subsidiary to others listed above.

Americans

The MACV province team (Military Assistance Command, Vietnam) numbers about forty men in Vinh Long city plus five-man units in each of the seven districts in the province. The MACV team includes mail clerks, mess sergeants, and maintenance men who also serve the dozen or so American civilians stationed in Vinh Long. The American civilians help channel United States aid materials into the province, and they advise South Vietnamese civilian officials in such areas as agriculture, education, public works.

Viet Cong

An estimated 6000 Viet Cong troops are operating in Vinh Long province, including elements of three battalions (total: 1200 men),[3] seven company-size District Concentrated Units (total: 500 men), about 1100 village guerrillas; the remainder are irregulars. In addition, an unknown and unevaluated number of Viet Cong political cadre are at work.

Viet Cong strength is centered in Vung Liem, Tam Binh, and Tra On districts on either side of the Mang Thit–Nicolai waterway. To quote from a document by the U.S. advisory staff:

"Active rebellion against central authority has been a tradition in these [three] districts . . . since the late 1940s, and even earlier in some villages. Certain families are said to have had grandfathers who led peasant revolts against the

[3] Only one battalion has all its units committed in Vinh Long. The other two battalions have some units in Vinh Long and some units in adjacent provinces.

French in the 1920s, father [sic] a Viet Minh cadreman, and now sons in the Viet Cong."

A United States estimate in mid-1967 placed 94,000 Vinh Long inhabitants — about one-fifth the province population — under firm Viet Cong control, with at least that many more living in "contested" areas. The breakdown by hamlets was:

GVN control: 172
Contested: 61
Viet Cong: 52

Appendix B

Statistics pertinent to the battle on Easter Sunday[1]

CASUALTIES

U.S.	ARVN	Viet Cong
4 killed in action	24 KIA	184 KIA (plus estimated 100
12 wounded in action	69 WIA	dead carried away)
		2 captured

U.S.–ARVN WEAPONS LOST

1 M–1 rifle, 1 .45-caliber pistol

VIET CONG EQUIPMENT CAPTURED

Weapons

2 BARs
2 Chinese light machine guns
6 Russian rifles
5 U.S. M–1 rifles
8 U.S. M–1 carbines
1 U.S. M–2 carbine
3 Russian AK–47 rifles
1 Czech light machine gun

4 SKS rifles
3 flare pistols
5 pistols
2 U.S. Thompson submachine guns
2 Russian B–40 rocket launchers
1 U.S. .82-mm. mortar sight

[1] Statistics courtesy 9th ARVN Division, Sadec; 7th U.S. Air Force, Saigon; 13th U.S. Army Aviation Bn., Can Tho.

Miscellaneous

12 magazines	Bugle
1 PR 7 x 50 binoculars	Documents
Sampan motors	

Communications

1 PRC–10 radio, U.S.	1 tripod (GRC–87)
3 telephones, Chinese	15 miles communications wire
2 telephones (TA 312)	1 light set and generator
2 switchboards, Chinese	

Ammunition

10 B–40 rockets	2 2/5 kilo mines
1700 rounds 7.62	1 10 Kilo mine
1000 rounds M1	1 57 RR round
1200 rounds LMG	2 ½ lb. TNT blocks
33 grenades	25 pistol flares

TASK ORGANIZATION

Division Control	*Task Force 16*	*Reserves*
9th Recon Co.	Hq 16th Regt.	2/16 Inf.
3/2 Cav. Trp.	2/16 Inf. Bn.	(committed)
	3/16 Inf.	43rd Rngr. Bn.
	43rd Rngr. Bn.	(committed)
	1/14 Inf.	2/14 Inf.
	2/2 Cav. Trp.	2/16 Inf.
	1 RF Co. (Vinh Long regional forces).	

Total ARVN forces engaged: 1900
Estimated No. VC engaged: 500

SUPPORTING FORCES

I. *Air Force*

Aircraft: AC–47, F–100, B–57, F–5, F–4C, A1H, O1E.

Sorties: 28 sorties Tactical Air, United States, Air Force
15 sorties Tactical Air, Vietnamese Air Force
9 Spooky patrols
continuous O1E FAC coverage

Ordnance: 57,000 pounds general purpose bombs
28,000 pounds napalm
3640 lbs. fragmentation-type bombs
16 canisters CBU — cluster bomb units
8 rocket pads, 6–8 2.75 rockets each
148,000 rounds 7.62-ammo (Spooky's Gatling guns)
231 Spooky flares, 2 million candlepower each
untotaled no. 20-mm. cannon rounds from all aircraft

II. *U.S. Army Aviation*
Aircraft: 43 UH1D transports (slicks)
29 UH1B armed helicopters (gunships)
4 dustoffs
2 C&C
1 CH–47
2 O1E
2 O1F

Sorties: 1161

Ordnance: 359,000 rounds 7.62
2352 rounds 2.75
1355 rounds 40 mm.

Three helicopters were destroyed in LZ Alpha. Another ship hit over target crashed en route back to Vinh Long. Jerry Daley managed, in his stubborn way, to guide his ventilated smoke ship back to base, but Major Millward pronounced it beyond repair. Twelve other helicopters suffered repairable damage.

Did you find these statistics interesting? Why?

Appendix C

On a visit to Saigon one day in May 1967, just after the much-heralded nationwide village elections, I came upon a bundle of back issues of the French magazine, Indochine Sud Est Asiatique. *They were published in 1953. Here are excerpts.*

The transport squadrons of the Army Air Force in Indochina have, since October 1952, flown 8 million kilometers. They have registered 25,261 sorties, carried 24,400 tons of cargo and 143,000 passengers, and they have dropped 75,000 paratroopers.

"I was struck by the high morale of the Vietnamese soldiers, the intelligence of the officers who command them, and above all the new fact that the population is joining in in the struggle against the terrorists."
> — French President Paul Reynaud in Saigon,
> summing up an inspection trip.

"What we need is time, men, and a workable administration."
> — General Di Linares in an interview.

The Na San airport is now handling more traffic than [the Paris airports] Orly or Bourget.

Each year sees a refinement of military tactics in Indochina . . . Since the fall of Nghia-Lo, isolated outposts have been downgraded. The latest tactic involves hedgehopping airmobile units.

Vietnam has now successfully completed an extraordinary undertaking: In the midst of a violent civil war . . . the government has conducted village elections employing every guarantee of liberty and independence of choice that can be imagined for any modern State . . . One need only recall the old Vietnamese saying, "The authority of the King stops at the gates of the village," to appreciate the full significance of these elections . . .

Nevertheless, certain observers have tended to write off the elections as being . . . without political significance. This interpretation vastly underestimates the importance of the event. It should be emphasized that, in the weeks preceding the elections, the Viet Minh announced a two-pronged anti-election campaign: On the one hand, terrorism and sabotage would be stepped up; on the other hand, voters would be pressured into abstaining. Yet, despite these threats, not only did 80.21% of eligible voters participate in the election, but, equally significant, 15,000 candidates presented themselves for the 7000 seats at stake.

During a twenty-day period last November, French carrier-based aircraft unloaded 200 one-thousand-pound bombs, 313 five-hundred-pound bombs, 200 two-hundred-sixty-pound bombs, 81 two-hundred-fifty-pound bombs, 228 rockets, 19,500 rounds of .20-mm. cannon, and 110,000 12.7 machine gun rounds.

Appendix D

In July 1967, Defense Secretary McNamara went on one of
his periodic fact-finding missions into South Vietnam.

During the July trip, McNamara visited the U.S. Special
Forces camp in My An, just north of Vinh Long. There he
obtained a firsthand report from General Thi on how things
were going in the 9th ARVN Division tactical area. I managed to obtain a transcript of General Thi's briefing. The
transcript follows.

I am going to confine my briefing to one particular aspect of
the RD program in the (9th) division tactical area. That is
the opening of the Mang Thit River/Nicolai Canal.

1. Characteristics of the Mang Thit River

The Mang Thit River, which was extended to connect
the Bassac and the Mekong Rivers early in the 20th century, is one of the most important waterways in the Delta.

This 30-mile waterway reduced by 2½ days the time required for rice barges to get from the Southern provinces
of the Delta to Saigon.

Viet Cong actions along the waterway in 1963 closed it

to commercial traffic. The heavy costs of the longer route to Saigon rendered rice shipment from the Delta to Saigon uneconomic and contributed to rice shortages in other areas of the Republic of Vietnam.

The reopening of the Mang Thit River will influence both the economic and military situations in the Delta:

a. For the economic, the reopening of the Mang Thit waterway will reduce the price of rice and other products of the Delta. The flow of supplies from the lower Delta to Saigon will not be limited to Highway No. 4 or the long water route to the north through An Giang province.

b. Militarily, the reopening of the Mang Thit waterway will reduce considerably the flow of VC supplies from the coast to the inner provinces. It also will cause the VC to mass in the Mang Thit area and will therefore make them more vulnerable to our search and destroy operations.

2. Government Effort in the Mang Thit River/Nicolai Canal area.

The government effort to reopen this waterway falls in two main categories: 1 — An active Revolutionary Development program. 2 — Strengthening the existing outposts and building additionally needed ones.

a. The RD program. Along the Mang Thit River, the RD program includes:

7 Ap Doi Moi (hamlets)

5 Ap Binh Dinh

The completion of this RD program will allow us to control about 15,000 people. To support this RD program, we have:

    5 RD cadre teams
    2 ARVN battalions
    3 Regional Force Companies
    4 Popular Forces Platoons
    1 NPFF Company
  b. Construction of outposts.
    In addition to the RD program, we have built 11 additional outposts and strengthened the old ones.
  c. Other support.
    We have also one River Assault Group which is operating on the waterway on a permanent basis. This valuable addition supports the effort by moving troops and supplies, by assisting outposts, by aiding in resources and population control, and by participating in military operations.

3. Military Operations.

    Communist opposition to the government offensive has been intense. At least one large VC unit has been diverted from another division tactical area with specific instructions to sabotage the government effort along the Mang Thit River. Harassment and attacks on outposts has been frequent.

    An important turning point came on Easter Sunday, March 26, 1967, when an estimated two VC battalions attacked a government element. They were firmly repulsed in the 9th Division's immediate reaction operation which followed the same day. The VC suffered 182 known dead by body count. Subsequent intelligence indicates VC casualties were much higher. Government casualties were 24 dead and 76 wounded.

    Since January 1, 1967, in the Mang Thit area alone, the VC casualties have totaled 395 confirmed KIA as compared to 82 friendly KIA.

4. Future progress.

There have been encouraging signs of progress. The RD hamlets have attracted numerous refugees from VC-held areas. Elements of the 9th Division conduct regular operations which serve as an effective deterrent to large scale communist attacks on the outposts and RD hamlets and which prevent the VC from massing any significant forces in the area. One of the documents we have captured shows that the VC are very much understrength. For instance, the 509 VC Battalion, which participated in the attack on Easter Sunday, is now only 124 men strong. There is evidence that the VC cannot recruit soldiers to reinforce its units.

On the other hand, sampans are traversing the waterway in increasing numbers. Enemy harassment has been reduced and VC taxation stopped.

The reopening of the Mang Thit waterway to commercial shipping represents a step of great significance to pacification and RD and to the government's effort to insure free commerce on its waterways.

Thus edified, Defense Secretary McNamara returned to Saigon for the night. The next morning he moved out into the field again for another firsthand report.

Appendix E

Jottings from a reporter's notebook, 1967–69.

If the war in Vietnam is to be characterized as a test of will, then it is important to differentiate between the Vietnamese concept of will and the American concept. American will is a kind of stubbornness, Vietnamese will is closer to patience. Stubbornness is dynamic, neurotic, heroic, creative. Patience is patient.

💥

In these times, the American leader who takes the nation into war on moral grounds — to meet what is described as a challenge to the American Way of Life — can be assured of strong internal opposition to his war. For it is a feature of these times that the American Way of Life is being challenged right here at home.

💥

Moreover: When our foreign policy becomes committed in advance to the defense of an abstract moral cause — be that cause as laudable as human rights or "self-determination" — we are in danger of being exploited. The danger surfaces when other governments, unfortunately committed only to their own naked interest, attempt to align their interest with our cause.

☙

Driven by a natural predilection for strategy (technical and precise), as opposed to diplomacy (shadowy and vague), American foreign policy makers have come to equate internationalism with technical involvement. From this, it follows that withdrawal of personnel means withdrawal into isolation. The concept is wrongheaded. The measure of a nation's role in international politics is not in the number of personnel it has stationed on foreign soil. The measure of a nation's role is in its power, its military flexibility, and its *diplomatic flexibility*. The absence of a proportionate dose of any one of those ingredients weakens the whole structure.

☙

Reform is a device for altering political, social, and economic conditions with a minimum of political, social, and economic disruption. It has some validity in America.

In America, I said.